COLLINS • LONGMAN

WORLD ATLAS

Editorial advisers
Stephen Scoffham, Colin Bridge, Terry Jewson

C O N T E N T S

CONTINENTS

A continent is a large mass of land.

There are seven continents in the world. Europe, Africa and Asia are joined together to make the largest land mass. North and South America are also linked, stretching most of the way from the North Pole to the South Pole. The other two continents, Oceania and Antarctica, stand on their own separated from the rest.

The earth from space

North America lies between the Atlantic and Pacific Oceans.

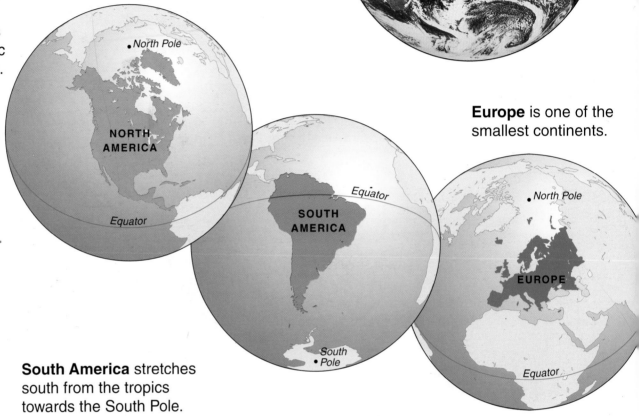

Europe is one of the smallest continents.

South America stretches south from the tropics towards the South Pole.

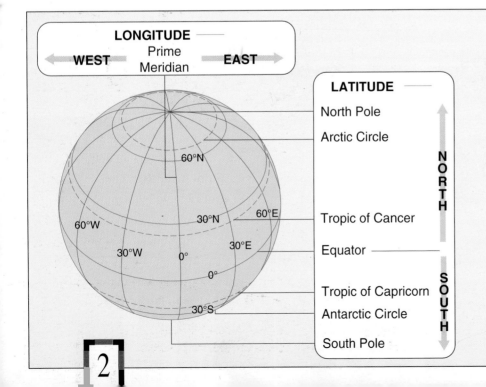

Latitude and longitude

The world is covered by two sets of imaginary lines:

1. Lines of latitude are circles around the earth. They are numbered in degrees north or south of the equator.

2. Lines of longitude are lines linking the North and South Poles. They are numbered in degrees east or west of a line through London, known as the Prime Meridian.

Using latitude and longitude people are able to describe where they are on the earth's surface.

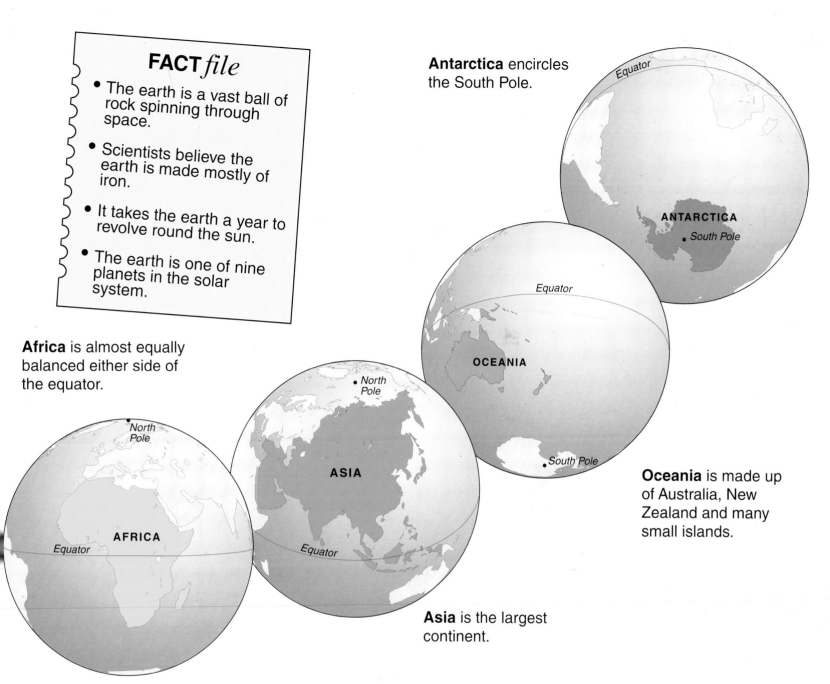

FACT *file*

- The earth is a vast ball of rock spinning through space.
- Scientists believe the earth is made mostly of iron.
- It takes the earth a year to revolve round the sun.
- The earth is one of nine planets in the solar system.

Africa is almost equally balanced either side of the equator.

Antarctica encircles the South Pole.

Oceania is made up of Australia, New Zealand and many small islands.

Asia is the largest continent.

Mapping the world

It is impossible to show the earth, which has a curved surface, accurately on a flat piece of paper. To get round this problem, geographers have invented a number of different mapping systems. These are known as projections.

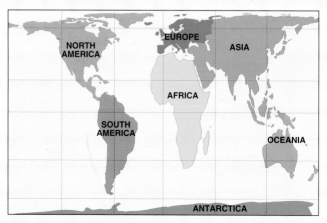

Peter's Projection shows area accurately but makes the continents the wrong shape.

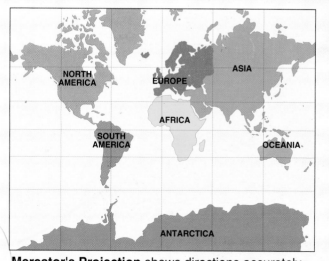

Mercator's Projection shows directions accurately, but makes the polar regions seem very large.

This atlas uses the Winkel projection. It shows area, shape and direction as accurately as possible.

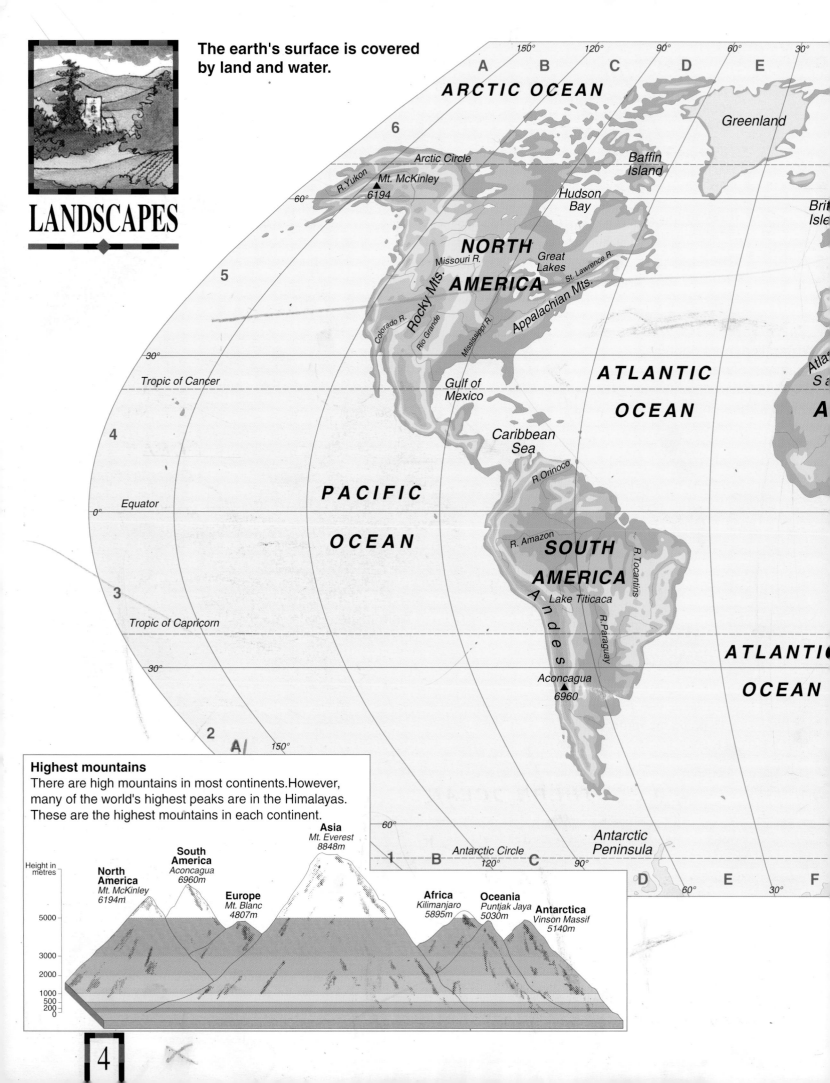

LANDSCAPES

The earth's surface is covered by land and water.

ARCTIC OCEAN

A B C D E

6

Greenland

Arctic Circle

Baffin Island

R.Yukon Mt. McKinley 6194

Hudson Bay

Brit Isle

NORTH AMERICA

Missouri R. Great Lakes St. Lawrence R.

Rocky Mts. Appalachian Mts.

Colorado R. Rio Grande Mississippi R.

30°

ATLANTIC OCEAN

Atl Sa

Tropic of Cancer

A

4

Gulf of Mexico

Caribbean Sea

PACIFIC OCEAN

R.Orinoco

Equator

0°

R. Amazon SOUTH AMERICA

R.Tocantins

Andes Lake Titicaca

R.Paraguay

3

Tropic of Capricorn

30°

ATLANTIC

OCEAN

Aconcagua 6960

2

A 150°

60°

Antarctic Peninsula

Antarctic Circle

1 B 120° C 90°

D E F

60° 30°

Highest mountains

There are high mountains in most continents. However, many of the world's highest peaks are in the Himalayas. These are the highest mountains in each continent.

Height in metres

Asia
Mt. Everest
8848m

South America
Aconcagua
6960m

North America
Mt. McKinley
6194m

Europe
Mt. Blanc
4807m

Africa
Kilimanjaro
5895m

Oceania
Puntjak Jaya
5030m

Antarctica
Vinson Massif
5140m

5000

3000
2000
1000
500
0

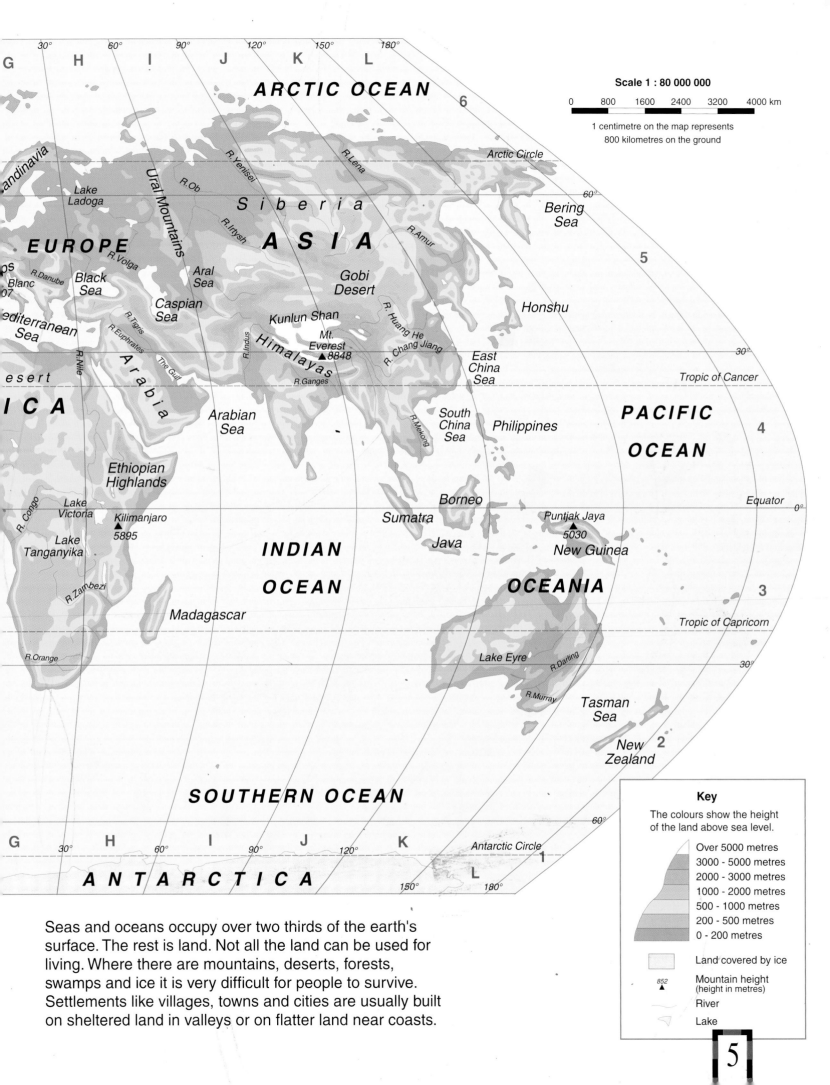

ARCTIC OCEAN

6

Scandinavia

R.Yenisei   R.Lena   Arctic Circle

Lake
Ladoga   R.Ob   60°

Ural Mountains   S i b e r i a   Bering
                                                  Sea

R.Irtysh

EUROPE   A S I A

R.Volga   Aral   Honshu   5
Blanc   R.Danube   Black   Sea   R.Amur
07   Sea   Gobi
        Caspian   Desert
editerranean   Sea
Sea   Kunlun Shan   30°
                                    R.Huang He
R.Tigris   Himalayas   Mt.   R.Chang Jiang   Tropic of Cancer
R.Euphrates   R.Indus   Everest
R.Nile   A   The Gulf   ▲8848   East
esert   r   China
        a   R.Ganges   Sea
ICA   b
        i   Arabian   South
                Sea   China   PACIFIC   4
                                    Sea   Philippines
                                                  OCEAN
        Ethiopian
        Highlands   R.Mekong
Lake   Equator
R.Congo   Victoria   Borneo   0°
        ▲Kilimanjaro   Sumatra   Puntjak Jaya
Lake   5895   ▲5030
Tanganyika   Java   New Guinea

R.Zambezi   INDIAN   OCEANIA   3

        Madagascar   OCEAN   Tropic of Capricorn

R.Orange   Lake Eyre   R.Darling   30°

                                    R.Murray   Tasman
                                              Sea
                                                  2
                                              New
SOUTHERN OCEAN   Zealand
                                                              60°

G   30°   H   60°   I   90°   J   120°   K   150°   L   180°   Antarctic Circle   1

A N T A R C T I C A   150°   180°

Seas and oceans occupy over two thirds of the earth's
surface. The rest is land. Not all the land can be used for
living. Where there are mountains, deserts, forests,
swamps and ice it is very difficult for people to survive.
Settlements like villages, towns and cities are usually built
on sheltered land in valleys or on flatter land near coasts.

Key

The colours show the height
of the land above sea level.

Over 5000 metres
3000 - 5000 metres
2000 - 3000 metres
1000 - 2000 metres
500 - 1000 metres
200 - 500 metres
0 - 200 metres

Land covered by ice

852
▲   Mountain height
        (height in metres)

River

Lake

5

RIVERS

Rivers shape the land as they flow towards the sea.

Rivers start as streams in hills and mountains. They flow down channels tumbling over waterfalls and cutting deeper and deeper valleys. The power of the water wears away the land. Rocks, gravel and sand are carried down stream. This is called erosion.

The Nile is the longest river in the world.

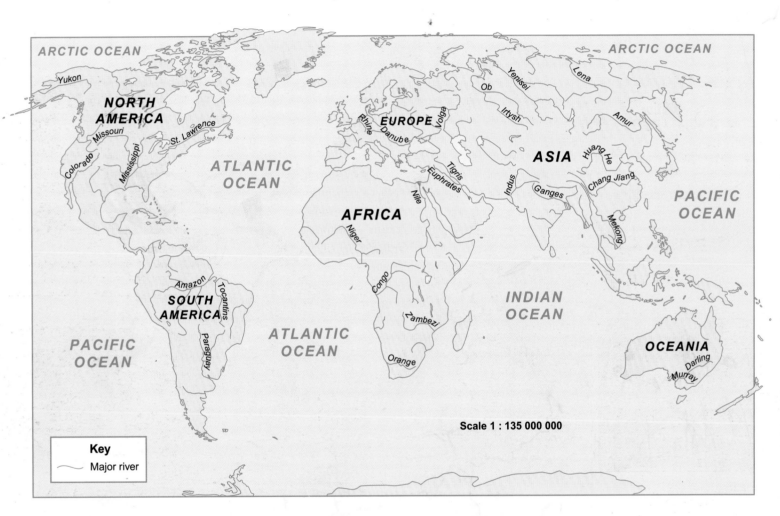

FACTfile - The longest river in each continent

RIVER	CONTINENT	SOURCE	MOUTH	LENGTH
Nile	Africa	Lake Victoria	Mediterranean Sea	6695 km
Amazon	South America	Andes	Atlantic Ocean	6570 km
Mississippi - Missouri	North America	Rocky Mountains	Gulf of Mexico	6020 km
Chang Jiang	Asia	Kunlun Shan	Pacific Ocean	5471 km
Murray-Darling	Oceania	Great Dividing Range	Indian Ocean	3717 km
Volga	Europe	Valdai Hills	Caspian Sea	3688 km

The River Rhine

The Rhine is one of the busiest rivers in the world. It rises in the Alps and flows 1320 km across Switzerland, Germany and the Netherlands to the North Sea.

There are many ancient towns on the banks of the Rhine. Some of these have grown into great industrial cities. At the mouth of the Rhine there is a large modern port called Europort. Barges and small ships travel up the Rhine as far as Basel in Switzerland. They carry coal, iron ore, steel, petrol and other heavy goods.

The Rhine also provides drinking water for 20 million people. This has to be cleaned very carefully to remove pollution from farms and factories.

Key

- 3000 - 5000 metres
- 2000 - 3000 metres
- 1000 - 2000 metres
- 500 - 1000 metres
- 200 - 500 metres
- 0 - 200 metres

- River
- Lake
- Country boundary
- • Town or city

Scale 1 : 4 200 000

0   42   84   126   168   210 km

Mouth and Delta
The river divides into a number of different channels and flows into the North Sea.

Gorge
The water cuts a deep valley through the hills.

Waterfall
The water tumbles over hard, steep rocks at Schaffhausen.

Tributaries
The Neckar, Main and Mosel join the Rhine.

Source
The river starts as melting ice from a glacier in the Alps.

Lake
Water fills the valley to make Lake Constance.

North Sea

NETHERLANDS

Europort
Rotterdam

GERMANY

Düsseldorf

Cologne

BELGIUM

Koblenz

R. Rhine

R. Mosel

R. Rhine

R. Main

LUXEMBOURG

Mainz

Strasbourg

R. Neckar

FRANCE

R. Rhine

Schaffhausen

Lake Constance

Basel

SWITZERLAND

A L P S

CLIMATE

There are different climates around the world.

Rainfall and temperature are the main elements that make up climate. Generally, the areas around the equator are the hottest places and North and South Poles the coldest. Rain does not fall so evenly around the world. It depends on the direction of the wind and the height of the land.

You can use the map to find out about the climate in different places in the world. Which climate do you think covers the largest area?

POLAR CLIMATE

Polar climates are the coldest on earth. In winter it is dark most of the time. Even in the summer the sun is weak. It hardly ever rains but there are many snow storms and blizzards. Few plants can grow in these conditions.

DESERT CLIMATE

Desert climates are extremely dry. Some deserts such as the Sahara, are very hot because they are close to the equator. Others, like the Gobi, are cold. Only a few tough plants manage to survive in such harsh conditions.

TROPICAL CLIMATE

Tropical climates have two seasons - one wet, one dry. The dry season is very hot. When the rains come they can bring violent storms turning dusty tracks into rivers. Wide areas of grassland are found here, often with scattered gnarled and thorny trees.

EQUATORIAL CLIMATE

Equatorial climates have no seasons and the weather is often cloudy and humid. Plants flourish as it is hot and wet throughout the year. In the rainforests there are huge trees, fast-growing shrubs and exotic plants.

World climate

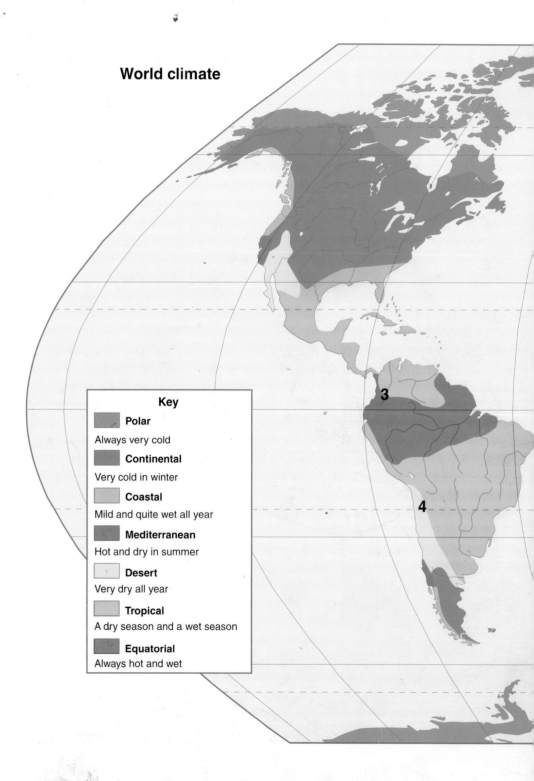

Key

- **Polar**
  Always very cold
- **Continental**
  Very cold in winter
- **Coastal**
  Mild and quite wet all year
- **Mediterranean**
  Hot and dry in summer
- **Desert**
  Very dry all year
- **Tropical**
  A dry season and a wet season
- **Equatorial**
  Always hot and wet

CONTINENTAL CLIMATE

Continental climates have big changes in temperature. The winters are extremely cold but the summers can be hot. There is rain throughout the year which is thundery in summer. Great conifer forests are found here.

COASTAL CLIMATE

Coastal climates are generally mild and quite wet. There are four seasons - spring, summer, autumn and winter - and a great variety of weather. Most of the rain comes in the winter. Many plants grow in these areas.

MEDITERRANEAN CLIMATE

Mediterranean climates have hot, dry summers. Most of the rain falls in the winter but there is hardly any frost or snow. Many colourful and attractive plants such as these poplar trees grow in Mediterranean areas.

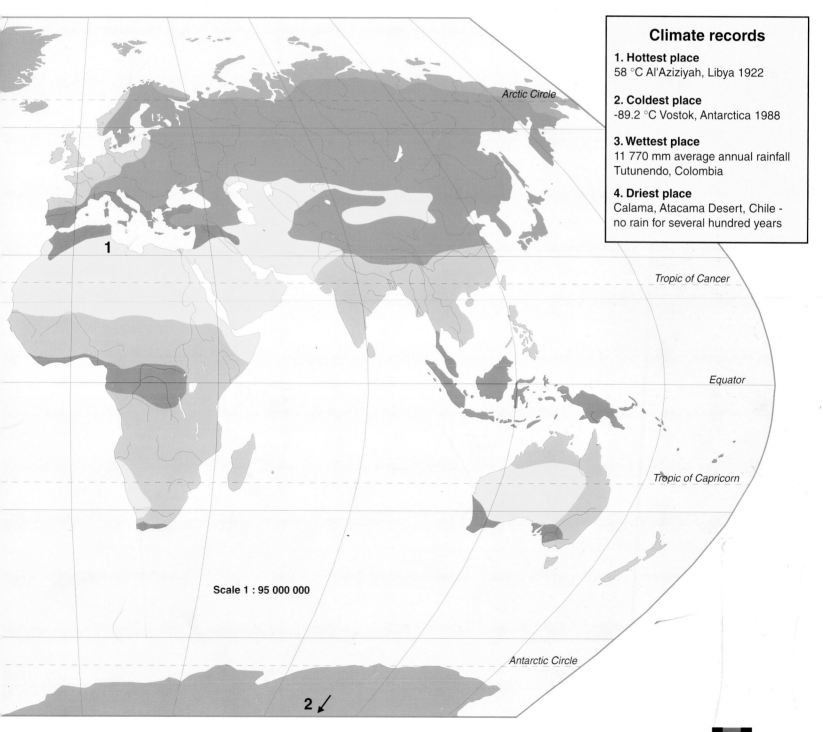

Arctic Circle

Tropic of Cancer

Equator

Tropic of Capricorn

Antarctic Circle

Scale 1 : 95 000 000

Climate records

1. Hottest place
58 °C Al'Aziziyah, Libya 1922

2. Coldest place
-89.2 °C Vostok, Antarctica 1988

3. Wettest place
11 770 mm average annual rainfall Tutunendo, Colombia

4. Driest place
Calama, Atacama Desert, Chile - no rain for several hundred years

NATURAL HAZARDS

There are five main types of natural hazards - droughts, storms, floods, earthquakes and volcanoes.

Natural hazards can affect people in all parts of the world. You can see from the map the areas of the world which are most at risk.

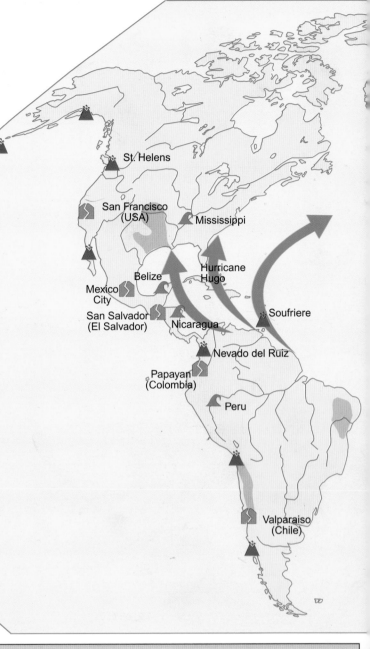

St. Helens

San Francisco (USA)

Mississippi

Belize

Hurricane Hugo

Mexico City

San Salvador (El Salvador)

Nicaragua

Soufriere

Nevado del Ruiz

Papayan (Colombia)

Peru

Valparaiso (Chile)

Storms

Storms can uproot trees and blow down houses. The worst storms affect the tropics. Here cyclones bring terrible gales with winds of over 120 km per hour. They are known as hurricanes in America and typhoons in Asia.

Hurricane Hugo was one of the worst recent storms. It swept across the Caribbean in September 1989 making thousands of people homeless and devastating crops.

Volcanoes

A volcano occurs where hot rock from deep within the core of the earth breaks through the surface. Most of the time volcanoes are harmless but they can sometimes erupt with enormous force.

In 1980 Mount St Helens in the USA exploded, blowing rock and gas into the sky. The sun was blocked out and dust was swept around the world in the upper atmosphere.

Earthquakes

Sometimes different parts of the earth's crust slip against each other causing a sudden shock. This is called an earthquake. If it happens near a town or city it can do very serious damage.

In January 1995 the city of Kobe in Japan was struck by a powerful earthquake. Over 5000 people were killed. Roads were twisted and thousands of homes were destroyed.

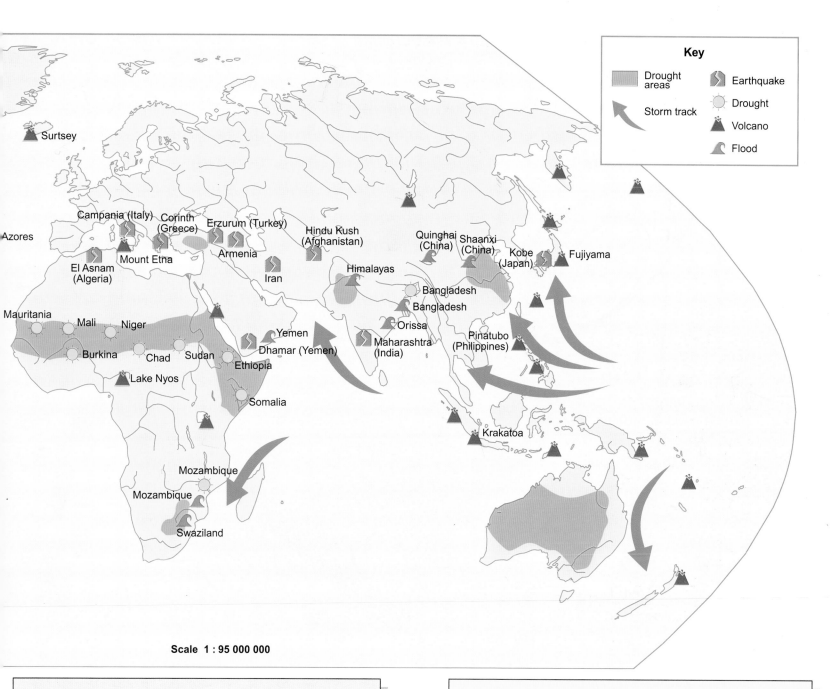

Key

Drought areas		Earthquake	
Storm track		Drought	
		Volcano	
		Flood	

Surtsey

Azores

Campania (Italy)

Corinth (Greece)

Erzurum (Turkey)

Hindu Kush (Afghanistan)

El Asnam (Algeria)

Mount Etna

Armenia

Iran

Himalayas

Quinghai (China)

Shaanxi (China)

Kobe (Japan)

Fujiyama

Mauritania

Mali

Niger

Burkina

Chad

Sudan

Ethiopia

Lake Nyos

Somalia

Yemen

Dhamar (Yemen)

Bangladesh

Bangladesh

Orissa

Maharashtra (India)

Pinatubo (Philippines)

Krakatoa

Mozambique

Mozambique

Swaziland

Scale 1 : 95 000 000

Floods

Floods can be caused in different ways. Sometimes heavy rain makes rivers burst their banks. On other occasions earthquakes may stir up tidal waves or break the walls of dams and reservoirs.

Heavy rainfall in midwestern USA in the summer of 1993 resulted in the flooding of the Mississippi river. This caused severe damage to crops and homes.

Droughts

Long periods without any rain are known as droughts. They are particularly dangerous in hot countries where crops and animals need lots of water. Sometimes droughts last for years on end.

For the past 15 years poor rainfall in northeast Africa has caused serious drought. This, combined with war and poverty, has resulted in severe famines.

PEOPLE

There are now more people in the world than ever before.

Some parts of the world are more crowded than others. In Europe, North America and Japan for example, many people live in big cities. China and India also have huge numbers of people. Elsewhere there are large empty areas where harsh conditions make it more difficult to survive.

Population growth

The world's population is growing larger all the time. We all need food, clothes and somewhere to live. Providing for these things is one of the most serious problems facing the world at the moment.

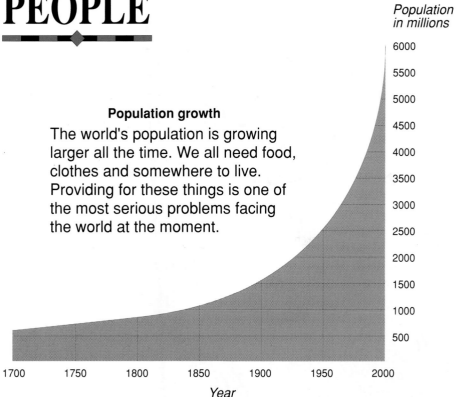

Population in millions

6000
5500
5000
4500
4000
3500
3000
2500
2000
1500
1000
500

1700 1750 1800 1850 1900 1950 2000

Year

Where people live

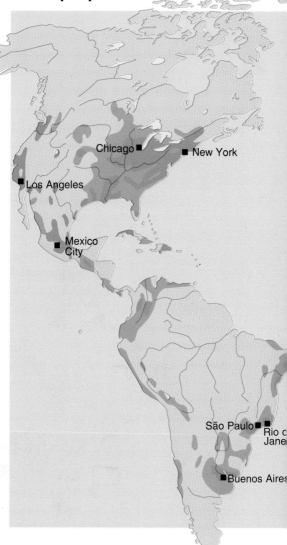

Chicago ■   ■ New York
■ Los Angeles
■ Mexico City
São Paulo ■ ■ Rio d Jane
■ Buenos Aires

Bigger and bigger cities

Across the world many people have moved to cities in search of a better life. Mexico City has doubled its population since 1970. It is expected to become the biggest city in the world by the year 2000.

Population in millions

30

20

10

0

MEXICO CITY   SAO PAULO   NEW YORK   BOMBAY   CAIRO   LONDON

Key
2000
1985
1970
Year

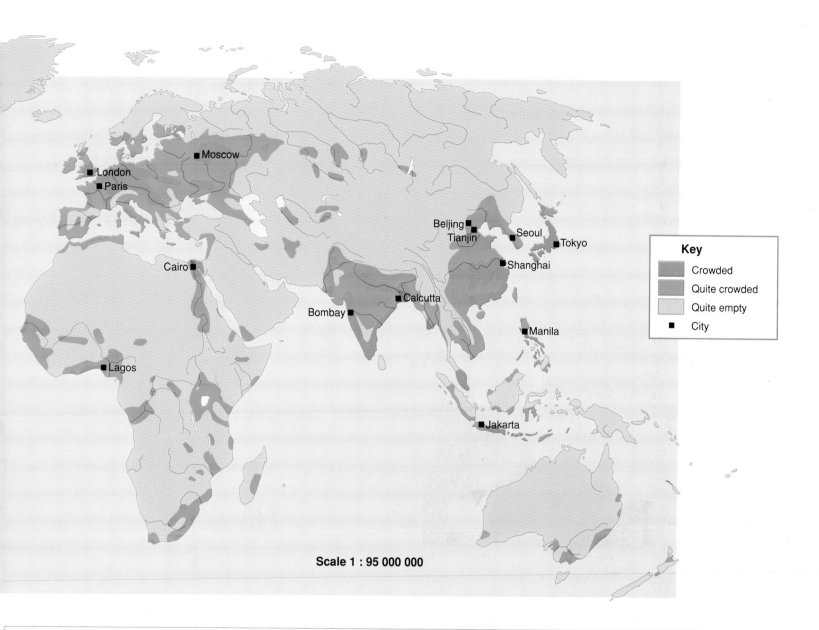

Scale 1 : 95 000 000

Key

Crowded
Quite crowded
Quite empty
■ City

WHY DO PEOPLE MOVE?

War

Parts of the world have been devastated by wars. The people who try to escape to safer places where they can live in peace are called refugees.

Work

People also move from one country to another in search of work. Some of them return home after a number of years. Others stay to form new communities.

Disasters

Droughts, floods and other disasters can drive people out of their homes. Poor people are especially badly affected as they have no money to spare for emergencies.

A new life

Sometimes people decide to move to a new country to retire or to set up a new home.

13

PLACES

Towns and cities can be sorted into groups or categories.

Towns and cities develop in different ways. The way that spaces and buildings are used gives a settlement its character.

Towns and cities are always changing but there are usually clues about their origins. Some places are important for trade. Others are centres for industry, leisure or government.

INDUSTRIAL CITY
Detroit has grown up as a manufacturing centre. In the past, coal provided the energy for the iron and steel industry. Today Detroit is a world centre of the car industry.

Key Features
Steel works, car factories.

Key

⏚	Port
✕	Crossing point
♖	Historic city
⛭	Industrial city
▤	New city
$	Financial centre
☀	Resort

NEW CITY
Brasília was created as a brand new capital city on open land in the south of Brazil. It is laid out on a grid with grand avenues, statues and fountains.

Key Features
Offices, shopping malls, government buildings.

RESORT

People are attracted to Monte Carlo for leisure and pleasure. It is famous for Grand Prix motor racing, fashion and yachting.

Key Features
Sun, sea, beaches, attractive scenery.

CROSSING POINT

Istanbul lies on the main routes between Europe and Asia. It is an important centre for trade and commerce.

Key Features
Large covered market, bridges, good road, rail and sea routes.

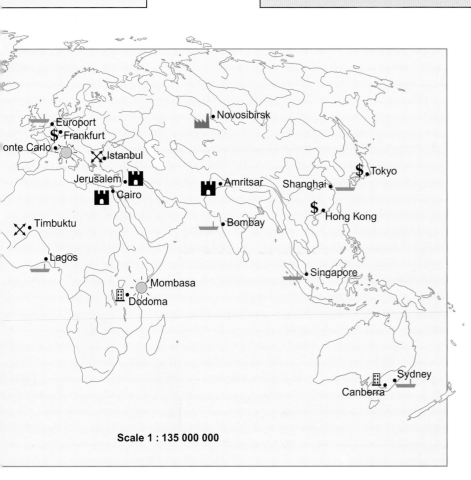

Scale 1 : 135 000 000

FINANCIAL CENTRE

Tokyo is famous world wide for its banks, stock exchange and insurance companies. Thousands of people work in offices handling money.

Key Features
Tall new office blocks, international computer and telephone links.

HISTORIC CITY

Jerusalem is one of the oldest cities in the world. It is a holy place for Christians, Jews and Muslims.

Key Features
Ancient buildings, old city walls, places of worship.

PORT

Singapore is one of the chief ports in Southeast Asia. Large ships collect and deliver goods from all over the world.

Key Features
Deep water harbour, warehouses.

SETTLEMENT

Chinon

FRANCE

Settlements develop for different reasons.

CHINON

Chinon is an ancient town in the west of France. It grew up at the lowest crossing point on the river Vienne. In the twelfth century the king built a great castle on the hill above the river. In the fifteenth century large stone houses were built by merchants.

Today Chinon has a population of about 9 000 people and the town has spread out on flat ground along the river bank. The town has several churches, a railway station, college and hospital. There is a street market every Thursday which attracts people from the surrounding area.

How is Chinon changing?

- A new trading estate has been built on the hill to the north of the town.

- There is a large nuclear power station ten kilometres away on the river Loire where many people work.

- In the summer Chinon is crowded with tourists who come to see the ancient buildings, visit the museums and buy the local wine.

| Castle on rocky hill provides defence from attack. | Houses built on flat land along the river bank. | Bridge uses island to cross the river. |

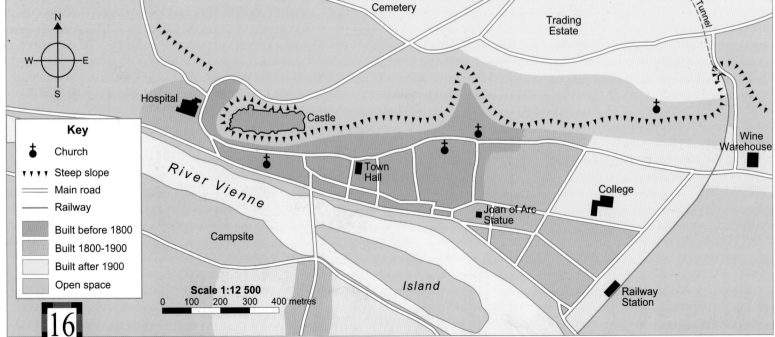

Key

- ✝ Church
- ▾▾▾▾ Steep slope
- ═══ Main road
- ─── Railway
- Built before 1800
- Built 1800-1900
- Built after 1900
- Open space

Scale 1:12 500

0   100   200   300   400 metres

Bombay

Bombay is a great city on the west coast of India. It is built on land which juts out into the sea. Nearly five hundred years ago the Portuguese traded goods here. Nowadays Bombay is a major international centre.

Bombay has good air, sea, road and rail links with other places. This is good for industry and attracts people from the surrounding area. In 1980 the population was about eight million. Numbers are expected to double by the year 2000.

BOMBAY

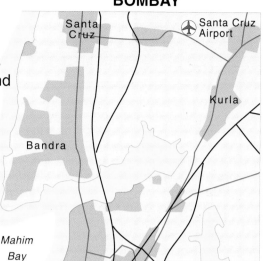

Map labels: Santa Cruz, Santa Cruz Airport, Kurla, Bandra, Mahim Bay, Fort, Salt Pans, Oil tanks, Arabian Sea, Stadium, Racecourse, Victoria Gardens, Bombay Harbour, Mahalaxmi Temples, Hospital, Docks, Cross Island, Towers of Silence, Chowpatty Beach, Government House, Malabar Point, Back Bay, Churchgate Station, Victoria Terminus, Cathedral, Town Hall, University, Museum, Gateway of India, Observatory

Key
- City centre
- Other built-up areas
- Parks
- Main road
- Railway

Scale: 0 1 2 3km

Housing

Some people live in houses or flats, but nearly half have no proper home.

Administration

Government offices look after the affairs of Bombay and the surrounding area. Other countries also have offices here.

Employment

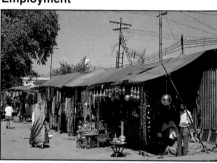

Some people have jobs in factories, but many others work for themselves.

Commerce

Offices and shops are crowded into the central area.

Transport

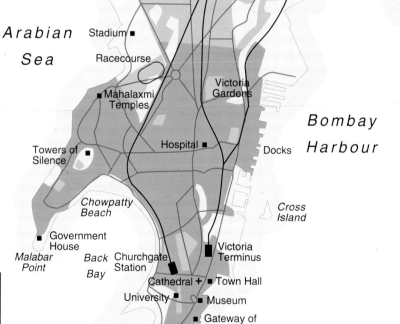

Many people use trains to travel to other parts of India.

Passenger and cargo planes

The Boeing 747 is the largest plane in use today and can carry 500 people. It is known as a "Jumbo Jet" because of its size.

Some aircraft only carry cargo. Letters, fruit and machine spare parts are sent by air when they have to be delivered quickly.

Concorde is the fastest plane in the world. It can fly at twice the speed of sound.

TRANSPORT

Air and sea routes link different countries of the world.

Main air routes

NORTH AMERICA
• Vancouver
San Francisco
• Denver
• Chicago
Newark • New York
Los Angeles
Tokyo
• Atlanta
Dallas/ Fort Worth
Sydney
Mexico City

EUROPE
London
Paris
Moscow
ASIA
Tokyo
Los Angeles
• Cairo
• Karachi
Hong Kong
• Bombay
Bangkok

AFRICA
• Nairobi
Singapore

SOUTH AMERICA
• Rio de Janeiro
• Buenos Aires

• Johannesburg

OCEANIA
Los Angeles
Sydney

Key
• Airport
— Main air route

Scale 1 : 135 000 000

Air transport is the quickest way of getting to distant places. The main routes are in Europe and North America. Chicago is the world's busiest airport with more than fifty million passengers per year - nearly as many as the entire population of the United Kingdom.

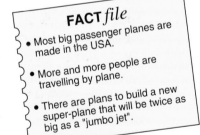

FACT *file*
• Most big passenger planes are made in the USA.
• More and more people are travelling by plane.
• There are plans to build a new super-plane that will be twice as big as a "jumbo jet".

Busiest airports TOP 10

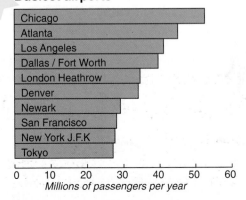

Chicago
Atlanta
Los Angeles
Dallas / Fort Worth
London Heathrow
Denver
Newark
San Francisco
New York J.F.K
Tokyo

0 10 20 30 40 50 60
Millions of passengers per year

How far and how long?

ROUTE	DISTANCE (kilometres)	AVERAGE JOURNEY TIME
London to Johannesburg	9 055	14 hours
2 London to New York	5 562	8 hours
3 Los Angeles to Tokyo	8 792	12 hours
4 Moscow to Tokyo	7 522	9 hours
5 New York to Rio de Janeiro	7 750	11 hours
6 Paris to Rio de Janeiro	9 168	13 hours
7 Singapore to Sydney	6 300	8 hours
8 Sydney to Los Angeles	12 062	17 hours

Passenger and cargo ships

The largest ships in the world are oil tankers. They can be up to half a kilometre long.

A container ship carries cargo in large boxes (containers) from one port to another.

Ferries are designed so that cars and lorries can drive straight on and off without delay.

Main shipping routes

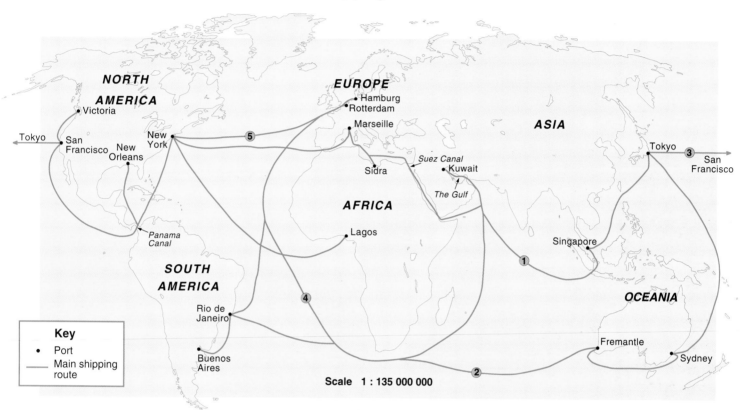

Key
- Port
— Main shipping route

Scale 1 : 135 000 000

FACT *file*
- The English Channel is one of the busiest seaways in the world.
- When it is moving at normal speed, an oil tanker takes several kilometres to stop.
- Many big ships are owned by international companies and their cargoes are worth millions of pounds.

Sea transport is the cheapest way of moving heavy goods. The busiest routes are between Japan and the industrial nations of Europe and North America. The Suez and Panama Canals provide ships with short-cuts between continents.

How far and how long?

ROUTE	DISTANCE (kilometres)	AVERAGE JOURNEY TIME
1 Kuwait to Tokyo	10 830	16 days
2 Rio de Janeiro to Fremantle	15 144	23 days
3 Tokyo to San Francisco	8 399	13 days
4 Sydney to Rotterdam	21 474	32 days
5 Hamburg to New York	6 547	10 days

Percentage of goods sent by sea

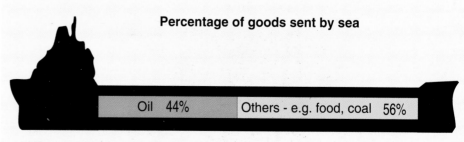

Oil 44%   Others - e.g. food, coal 56%

What goods do ships carry?

Oil makes up nearly half of all cargoes sent by sea. Much of the oil comes from The Gulf.

19

Farming is carried out in different ways around the world.

Some farms are made up of small patches of land that provide food for a single family. Other farms are much larger and are run as businesses selling crops or animals for a profit. What are the farms like near you?

FARMING

NORTH AMERICA
maize, wheat, sugar, soya beans

CEREAL FARMING
Harvesting wheat on the American Prairies.

Cereals are the world's most important food crops. They are usually ground into flour to make bread, pasta and other products. Main crops: wheat, maize, barley, oats.

RICE FARMING
Rice is grown in flooded fields known as paddies.

In Asia many people depend on rice for food. It needs a warm climate and plenty of water to grow well.

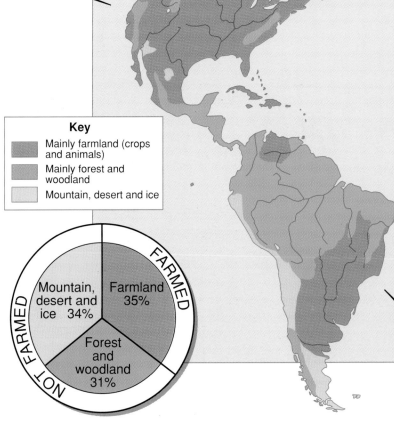

Key

- Mainly farmland (crops and animals)
- Mainly forest and woodland
- Mountain, desert and ice

FARMED

NOT FARMED

Mountain, desert and ice 34%

Farmland 35%

Forest and woodland 31%

Crops and animals can be farmed on only about a third of the world's surface. The rest is forested or covered by deserts, mountains, snow and ice.

ANIMAL FARMING
Sheep and cattle on an Australian ranch.

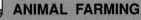

Animals are kept for their meat, milk and skins. They can graze land that is too dry to grow crops.
Main products : cattle, sheep, pigs.

FRUIT FARMING
Apple orchards are full of blossom in spring.

Many plants produce delicious fruits.
Main crops : grapes, bananas, oranges, apples.

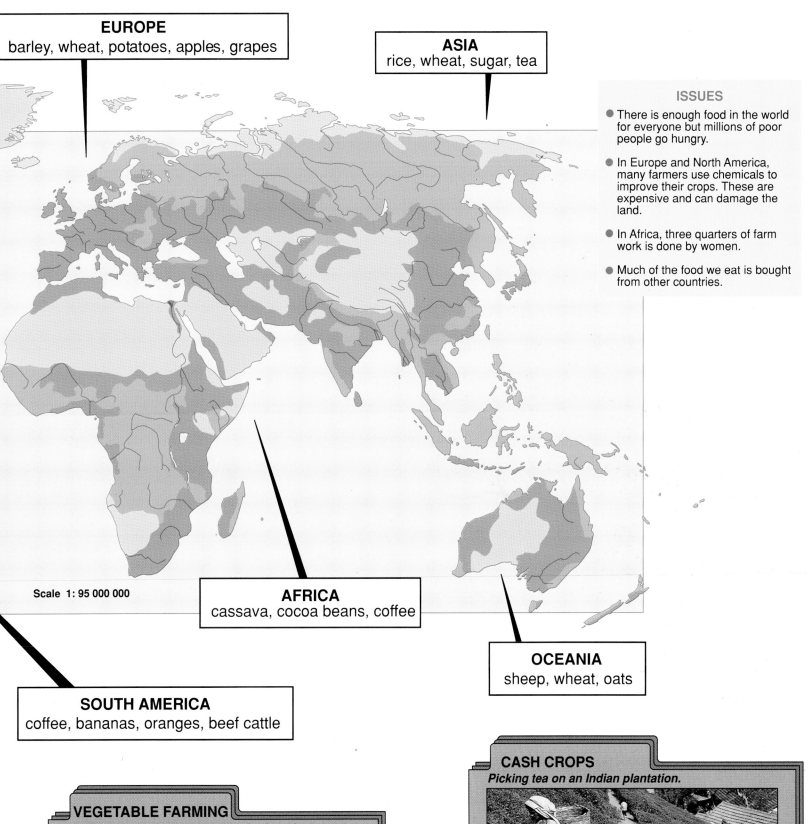

EUROPE
barley, wheat, potatoes, apples, grapes

ASIA
rice, wheat, sugar, tea

ISSUES

- There is enough food in the world for everyone but millions of poor people go hungry.

- In Europe and North America, many farmers use chemicals to improve their crops. These are expensive and can damage the land.

- In Africa, three quarters of farm work is done by women.

- Much of the food we eat is bought from other countries.

Scale 1 : 95 000 000

AFRICA
cassava, cocoa beans, coffee

OCEANIA
sheep, wheat, oats

SOUTH AMERICA
coffee, bananas, oranges, beef cattle

VEGETABLE FARMING
In Europe, market gardens can be found near towns.

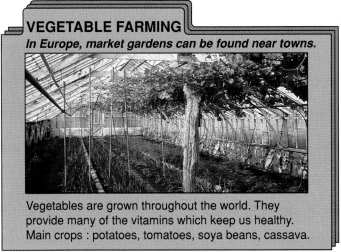

Vegetables are grown throughout the world. They provide many of the vitamins which keep us healthy.
Main crops : potatoes, tomatoes, soya beans, cassava.

CASH CROPS
Picking tea on an Indian plantation.

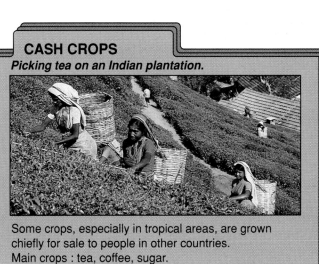

Some crops, especially in tropical areas, are grown chiefly for sale to people in other countries.
Main crops : tea, coffee, sugar.

Pollution is a problem that affects all parts of the world.

Why does pollution happen?
Sometimes pollution is the result of accidents. On other occasions it is built up over a period of time and nobody notices. Solving pollution problems can be very expensive. Most of them will leave their mark for years to come.

POLLUTION

2. Canada
Lakes poisoned by acid rain killing fish and other living creatures.

3. North Sea
Sewage and factory waste pollute the water.

4. Chernobyl
World's worst nuclear accident at Chernobyl in 1986 spreads radiation across Europe.

1. Alaska
Oil tanker runs aground in 1989 polluting long stretches of coast.

5. Aral Sea
Sea drying up and disappearing as rivers diverted into the desert to grow crops.

6. India
Accident at a chemical factory in Bhopal in 1984 poisons thousands of people.

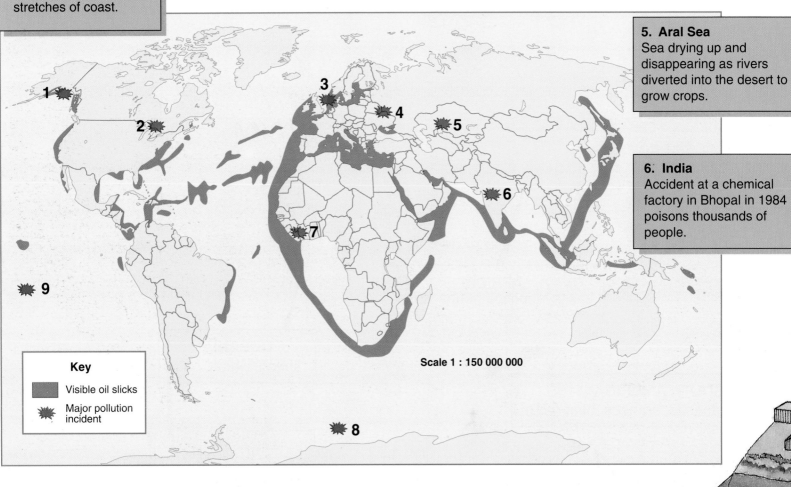

Scale 1 : 150 000 000

Key
Visible oil slicks
Major pollution incident

9. Pacific Islands
Nuclear bomb testing causes long-lasting contamination.

8. Antarctica
Hole in the ozone layer lets dangerous rays from the sun reach the earth's surface.

7. West Africa
Banned chemicals secretly dumped at open-air sites.

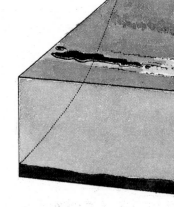

Causes of pollution

Cars cause a great deal of pollution. So too do power stations. Look carefully at this picture to see how many other sources of pollution you can discover.

Nuclear bomb tests
Radiation from nuclear bombs is especially dangerous as it is invisible and lasts for hundreds of years.

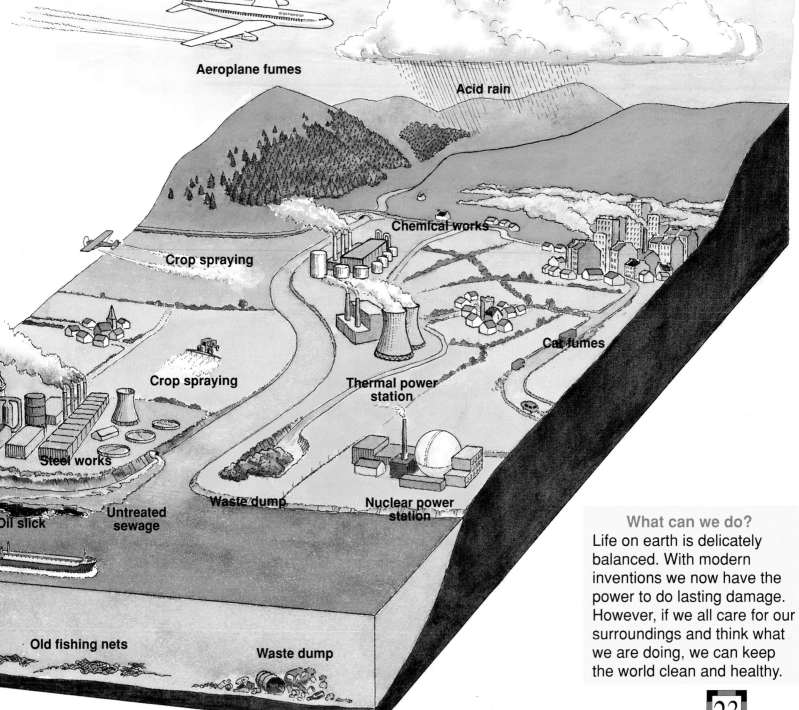

Aeroplane fumes

Acid rain

Chemical works

Crop spraying

Car fumes

Crop spraying

Thermal power station

Steel works

Oil slick

Untreated sewage

Waste dump

Nuclear power station

Old fishing nets

Waste dump

What can we do?
Life on earth is delicately balanced. With modern inventions we now have the power to do lasting damage. However, if we all care for our surroundings and think what we are doing, we can keep the world clean and healthy.

Acid rain
In northern Europe many trees have been killed by acid rain.

THREATENED ENVIRONMENTS

What people do affects the world we live in.

There are now more people living in the world than ever before.
However, our activities are starting to change the balance of life around the earth. To keep the world a pleasant place we need to be careful what we do.

Key

- Rainforest
- Edge of rainforest under threat
- Desert
- Fertile land which could turn to desert
- Northern forest
- Forests affected by acid rain
- Antarctica
- Sea / lakes

Rainforests

Nearly half the world's rainforests have already been cut down for farming or industry. As the trees are cleared, plants and creatures lose their homes and the soil washes away. The rainforests are the richest source of life on earth. People believe that we must do everything we can to save what remains.

Rainforests
Once the rainforest has been cleared the trees can never grow back again.

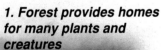

1. Forest provides homes for many plants and creatures

2. Trees cut down or burnt

3. Land used for ranching

4. Heavy rain washes away the soil

5. Land left empty and useless

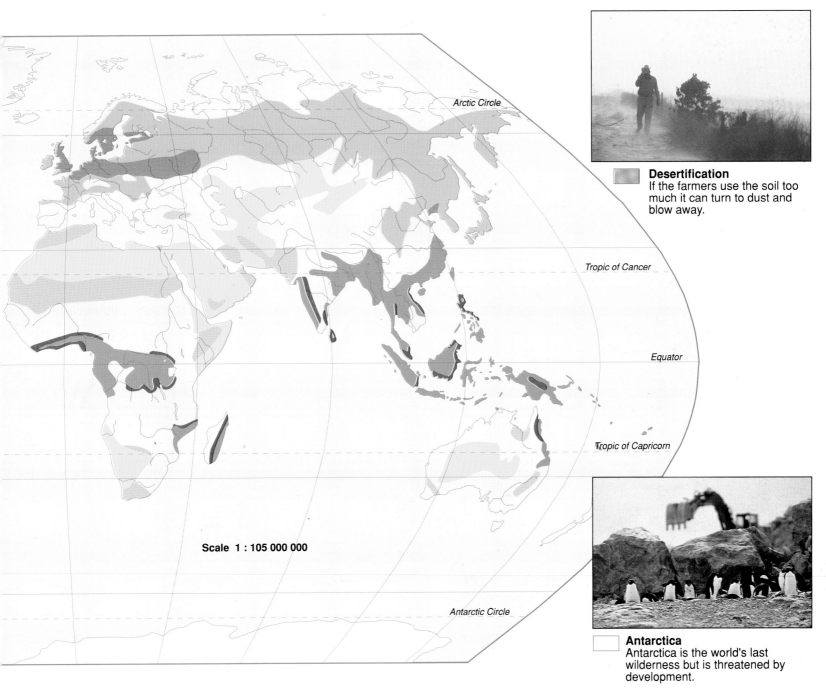

Arctic Circle

Tropic of Cancer

Equator

Tropic of Capricorn

Antarctic Circle

Scale 1 : 105 000 000

Desertification
If the farmers use the soil too much it can turn to dust and blow away.

Antarctica
Antarctica is the world's last wilderness but is threatened by development.

Global warming

Car fumes, factory smoke and other poisonous gases are building up in the air forming a blanket high above the earth. We now believe these are trapping heat from the sun. This is called global warming or the "greenhouse effect". If we use energy more efficiently, and develop alternative sources such as wind power, it should help to solve the problem.

What will happen if temperatures rise?

Nobody can be sure what will happen, but a lot of things will change. Some cold places may benefit. Dry areas will probably turn to desert. The sea level might rise around the world flooding coastlines. Storms could become worse.

heat bounces back into space

heat from the sun

burning fuel

some heat is trapped by greenhouse gases

aerosols

car fumes

fertilisers

NPK

Some sources of greenhouse gases

WATER

We all need clean water to stay healthy.

Half the people in the world do not have a safe supply of drinking water. This is a very serious problem as dirty water is the cause of many diseases.

The map shows the contrasts between different countries of the world. Areas away from towns are especially badly affected.

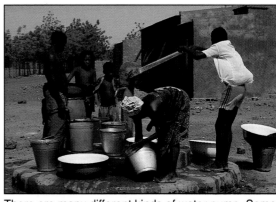

There are many different kinds of water pump. Some are worked by hand, others by foot.

Diseases from water

Diarrhoea

Diarrhoea is the most common cause of death in young children. It is caused by dirty water and unhealthy living conditions. Doctors have now discovered that this illness can be treated with a simple medicine made from salts and sugar.

5 million children under five years old die from diarrhoea each year.

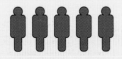

3.5 million could have been saved.

- Diarrhoea causes 10 million deaths a year.
- Half the deaths are children under five years old.
- Many of these lives could be saved.

Malaria

Some diseases are spread by insects which live in water. One of the worst is a fever called malaria. It is passed from person to person by mosquitoes, and is common in the tropics.

- Nearly 300 million people infected each year.
- 1 - 2 million deaths each year.
- Half the world's population at risk from infection.
- Tablets can prevent people getting malaria.

Tropic of Cancer

Tropic of Capricorn

Areas affected by malaria

Access to clean water

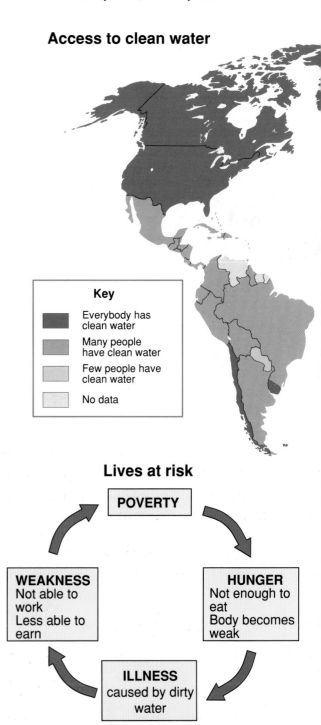

Key

- Everybody has clean water
- Many people have clean water
- Few people have clean water
- No data

Lives at risk

POVERTY

HUNGER
Not enough to eat
Body becomes weak

ILLNESS
caused by dirty water

WEAKNESS
Not able to work
Less able to earn

Poor people are especially at risk from disease. They get trapped in a cycle of events which is a danger to their lives.

In some parts of Africa women and children can spend five hours a day carrying water from the nearest well.

A litre of water weighs one kilogram. Many women carry twenty litres at a time.

Laying water pipes in Botswana.

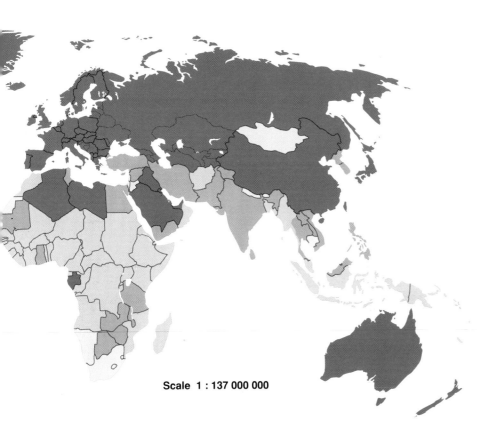

Scale 1 : 137 000 000

New storage tanks, Accra, Ghana.

Improving water supplies - Nicaragua

Around the world people are trying to improve water supplies. The best schemes are those that involve local people right from the start.

In Nicaragua, people in Boaco Province were using dirty water from damaged wells and pipes. A scheme was set up showing the locals how to make their own repairs. Village meetings were organised and the problems explained using books and videos. The water is now much better and the people are healthier.

Weeds should be cleared to remove places where flies and mosquitoes can breed.

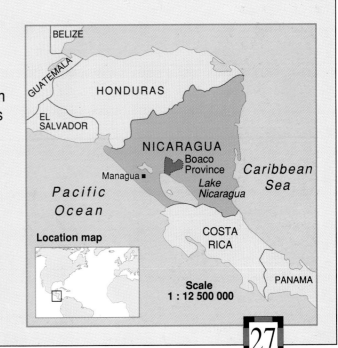

BELIZE
GUATEMALA
HONDURAS
EL SALVADOR
NICARAGUA
Boaco Province
Managua
Pacific Ocean
Lake Nicaragua
Caribbean Sea
COSTA RICA
PANAMA

Location map

Scale 1 : 12 500 000

UNEQUAL SHARES

ISSUES

● Only a quarter of the world's population lives in the north, but they consume three quarters of the world's resources.

● Women often work longer hours and are paid less for what they do than men.

● There are twice as many people in armies around the world as there are doctors, nurses and teachers.

The quality of life is known as welfare.

There are many different ways of measuring people's living standards. One way is to see if they have enough food to eat. Another is to find out how long they live. A third is to discover if they can read or write.

Look at the maps below. When you compare them you will see they each show a similar pattern. In the north there is a group of countries which have a high standard of living. In the south there is a group of countries which have a low standard of living. This difference between north and south is one of the main problems facing the world today.

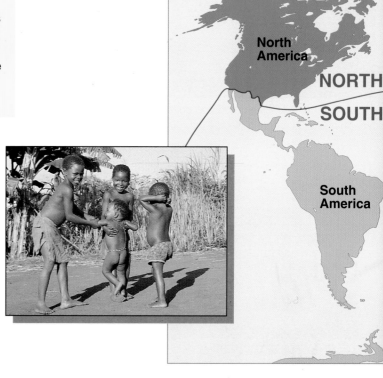

North America

NORTH

SOUTH

South America

FOOD

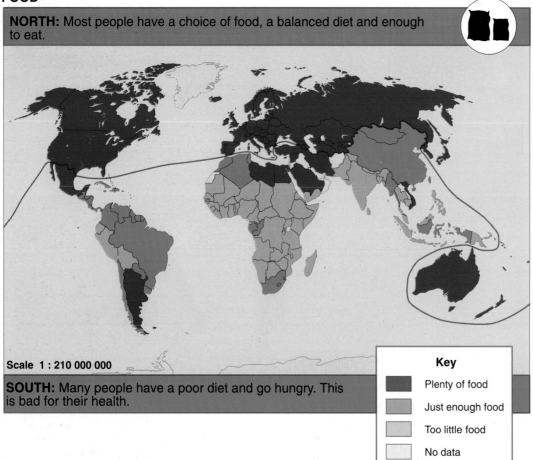

NORTH: Most people have a choice of food, a balanced diet and enough to eat.

Scale 1 : 210 000 000

SOUTH: Many people have a poor diet and go hungry. This is bad for their health.

Key

- Plenty of food
- Just enough food
- Too little food
- No data

LENGTH OF LIFE

NORTH: Most people can expect to live to nearly 75 years old.

Scale 1 : 210 000 000

SOUTH: Most people will die before they reach 60.

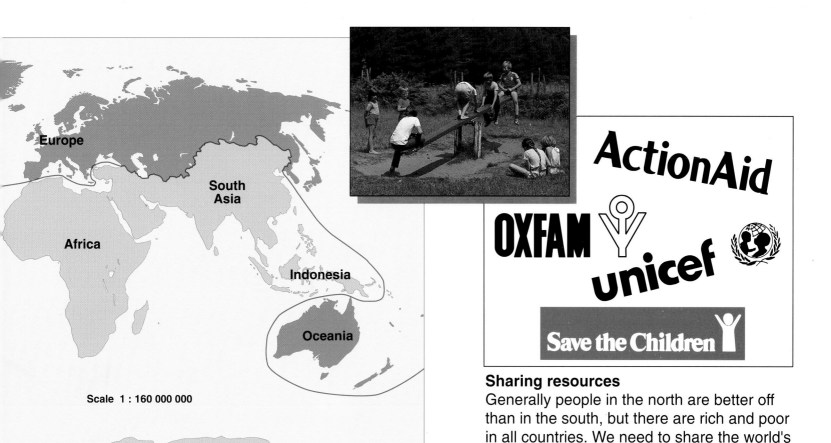

Europe

South Asia

Africa

Indonesia

Oceania

Scale 1 : 160 000 000

ActionAid

OXFAM

unicef

Save the Children

Sharing resources

Generally people in the north are better off than in the south, but there are rich and poor in all countries. We need to share the world's resources much more equally. Here are some of the organisations which help to do this.

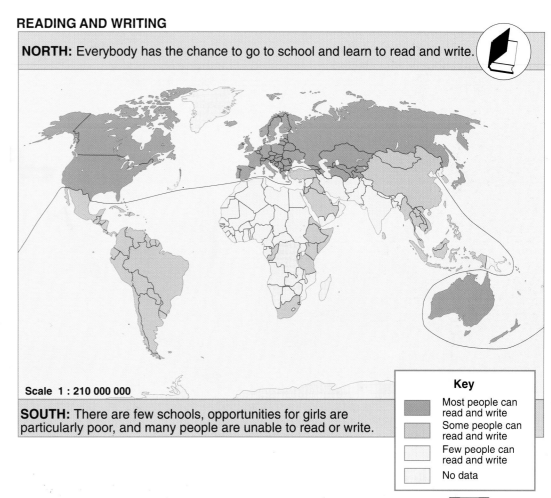

READING AND WRITING

NORTH: Everybody has the chance to go to school and learn to read and write.

Key

⬛	Over 70 years
▨	55 - 70 years
☐	Under 55 years
☐	No data

Scale 1 : 210 000 000

SOUTH: There are few schools, opportunities for girls are particularly poor, and many people are unable to read or write.

Key

⬛	Most people can read and write
▨	Some people can read and write
☐	Few people can read and write
☐	No data

CONSERVATION

Conservation projects care for places and things which seem important to the future of the world.

We are making more demands on the environment than at any time in history. Cities are getting larger, new industries are being set up, and more and more countryside is being used for farming. Many people are worried about what is happening. They believe we should be using our surroundings more carefully.

The map shows natural environments around the world. This page also tells you about five different conservation projects and has pictures of animals at risk.

FACT file

Conservation groups try to preserve and take care of the Earth. Examples include:
- Friends of the Earth
- Greenpeace
- WWF (Worldwide Fund for Nature)

Sometimes a group of countries decide to work together to solve a problem. Examples include:

- CITES - Convention of International Trade in Endangered Species
- IUCN - International Union for Conservation of Nature and Natural Resources

1. Natural wonders - Yellowstone National Park

The Rockies are a great chain of mountains stretching down the western coast of North America. One of the most beautiful areas is in Wyoming in the U.S.A. Here geysers and volcanic springs steam away among the conifer forests and snowy peaks.

The area attracts large numbers of visitors and has been made into a National Park. Special places around the world have been protected in the same way.

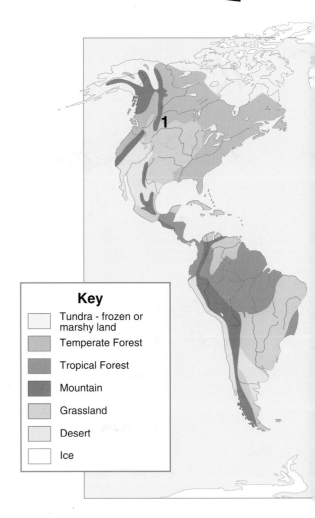

Key
- Tundra - frozen or marshy land
- Temperate Forest
- Tropical Forest
- Mountain
- Grassland
- Desert
- Ice

2. Preserving the Past - Venice

Venice is one of the world's most remarkable cities. It is built on an island in Northern Italy and is famous for its canals and beautiful buildings.

Now Venice is in danger. The buildings are sinking lower into the water. Pollution from factories and waves from ships are causing further damage. To preserve the city, people are planning to build a barrage which will protect it from the sea.

(Venice map key:)
Key
- Road
- Railway
- Canal

Mestre (mainland) · Venetian Lagoon · Murano · Venice · Lido · **VENICE**

Endangered Creatures

Whales - hunted for meat, oil and other products.

Parrots - caught and sold as pets.

3. Saving trees - The Sahel

In many parts of the world people depend on wood for heating and cooking. Some places suffer from shortages. The area south of the Sahara Desert, known as the Sahel, is particularly badly affected. Here the soil blows away as the trees are cut down.

Solar cookers and better stoves can help solve the problem. They are cheap enough for people to afford and help to save the trees that are left.

Natural Environments

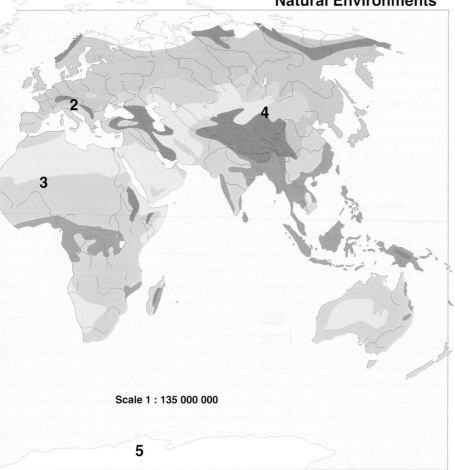

Scale 1 : 135 000 000

Elephants - shot for ivory.

Tigers - killed for their skins.

Turtles - captured for their meat, eggs and shells.

4. Protecting farmland - China

North West China is threatened by fierce winds from the Gobi desert. These can cover nearby farmland with sand and dust.

Recently the Chinese have been holding the desert back. They have put nets over the sand and built channels to bring water for the plants. As well as protecting farmland, some valuable new areas have been planted with crops.

5. World Park - Antarctica?

Antarctica is the world's last great wilderness. It is an empty land of snow and ice. Beneath the surface, however, there are large amounts of coal, oil and metal ore.

Many people would like to see Antarctica turned into a World Park. This would stop quarrels over resources and protect and preserve wildlife. The problem is that all countries will have to agree to co-operate.

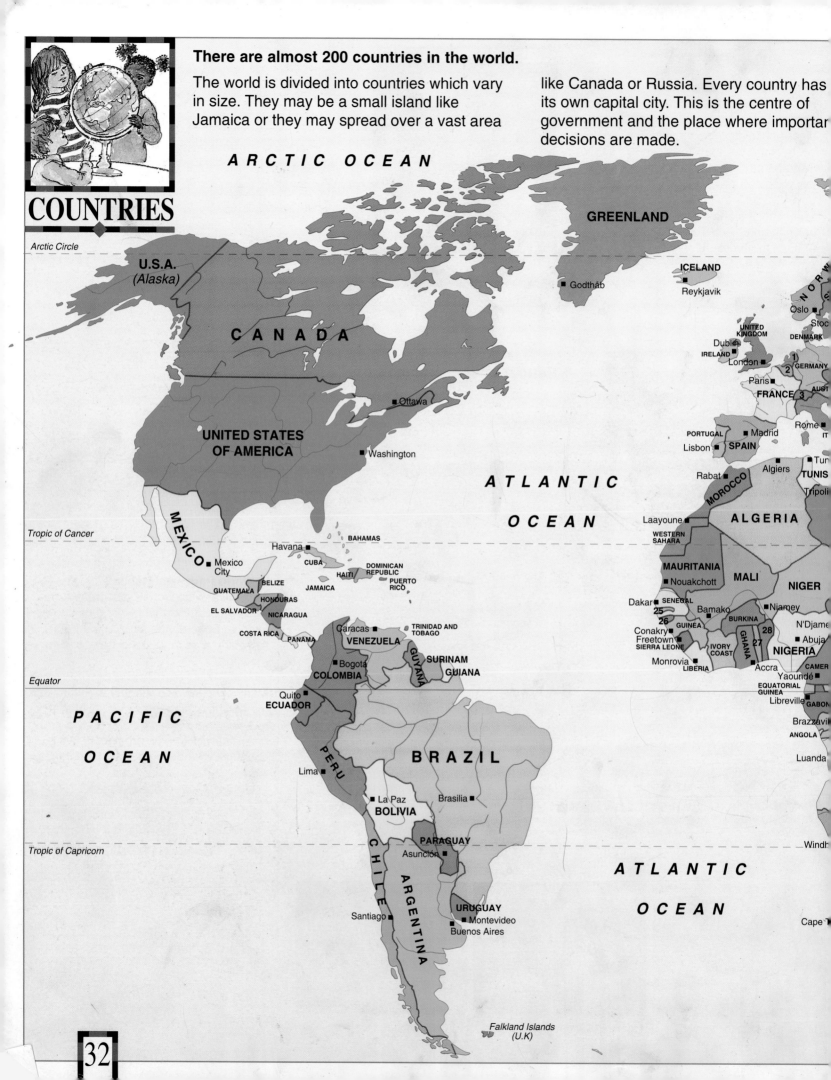

COUNTRIES

There are almost 200 countries in the world.

The world is divided into countries which vary in size. They may be a small island like Jamaica or they may spread over a vast area like Canada or Russia. Every country has its own capital city. This is the centre of government and the place where importan decisions are made.

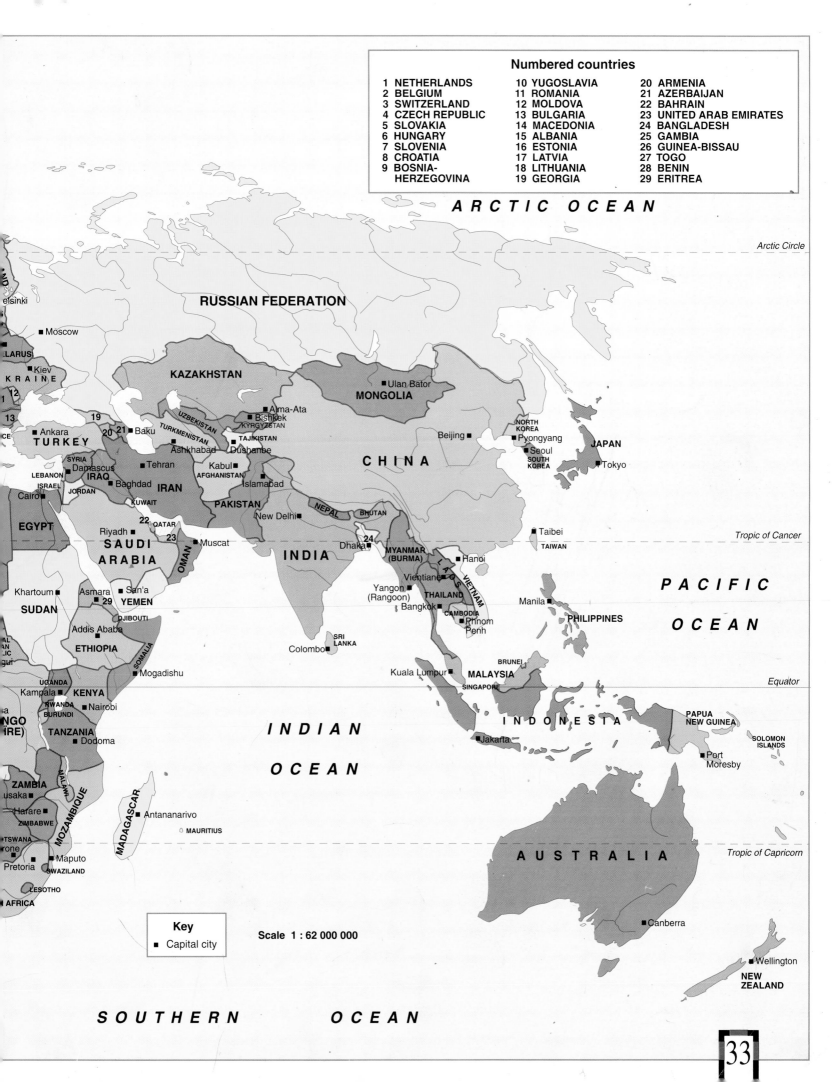

Numbered countries

1 NETHERLANDS	10 YUGOSLAVIA	20 ARMENIA
2 BELGIUM	11 ROMANIA	21 AZERBAIJAN
3 SWITZERLAND	12 MOLDOVA	22 BAHRAIN
4 CZECH REPUBLIC	13 BULGARIA	23 UNITED ARAB EMIRATES
5 SLOVAKIA	14 MACEDONIA	24 BANGLADESH
6 HUNGARY	15 ALBANIA	25 GAMBIA
7 SLOVENIA	16 ESTONIA	26 GUINEA-BISSAU
8 CROATIA	17 LATVIA	27 TOGO
9 BOSNIA-	18 LITHUANIA	28 BENIN
HERZEGOVINA	19 GEORGIA	29 ERITREA

ARCTIC OCEAN

Arctic Circle

elsinki

RUSSIAN FEDERATION

■ Moscow

■LARUS

■ Kiev

KRAINE

13

KAZAKHSTAN

19

■ Ulan Bator

MONGOLIA

1 12

Ankara

20 21 ■ Baku

TURKEY

■ Alma-Ata
■ Bishkek
KYRGYZSTAN

UZBEKISTAN

TURKMENISTAN

■ Beijing

NORTH
KOREA

JAPAN

■ Pyongyang
Seoul
SOUTH
KOREA

SYRIA
Damascus

■Tehran

Ashkhabad ■Dushanbe
TAJIKISTAN

CHINA

■ Tokyo

LEBANON
ISRAEL

IRAQ
■Baghdad

Kabul
AFGHANISTAN

IRAN

JORDAN

KUWAIT

Islamabad

Cairo■

PAKISTAN

■New Delhi

NEPAL

BHUTAN

■Taibei

Tropic of Cancer

EGYPT

22 QATAR

■ Riyadh

23

■ Muscat

Dhaka ■ 24

TAIWAN

**SAUDI
ARABIA**

OMAN

INDIA

**MYANMAR
(BURMA)**

■ Hanoi

PACIFIC

Khartoum ■

Asmara
29

■San'a

YEMEN

Vientiane ■

LAOS

VIETNAM

OCEAN

SUDAN

DJIBOUTI

Yangon
(Rangoon)

THAILAND

■ Manila

■Addis Ababa

SOMALIA

■Bangkok

CAMBODIA

■Phnom
Penh

PHILIPPINES

ETHIOPIA

SRI
LANKA

BRUNEI

UGANDA

Kampala ■

KENYA

■ Nairobi

Colombo ■

Kuala Lumpur ■ **MALAYSIA**

SINGAPORE

Equator

RWANDA
BURUNDI

NGO
RE)

TANZANIA

■ Dodoma

INDIAN

INDONESIA

**PAPUA
NEW GUINEA**

■Jakarta

SOLOMON
ISLANDS

OCEAN

■ Port
Moresby

ZAMBIA

MALAWI

usaka ■

MOZAMBIQUE

MADAGASCAR

■ Antananarivo

■Harare

◊ MAURITIUS

ZIMBABWE

TSWANA
one

Tropic of Capricorn

Pretoria ■

■Maputo

SWAZILAND

AUSTRALIA

LESOTHO

AFRICA ■

■Canberra

Key

■ Capital city

Scale 1 : 62 000 000

■Wellington

**NEW
ZEALAND**

SOUTHERN *OCEAN*

33

EUROPE

Key
- ■ Capital city
- • Other town or city
- — Country boundary
- Sea

BEL. : BELGIUM
B.H. : BOSNIA-HERZEGOVINA
LUX. : LUXEMBOURG
MAC. : MACEDONIA
NETH. : NETHERLANDS
R.F. : RUSSIAN FEDERATION
SL. : SLOVENIA
SWITZ. : SWITZERLAND

Scale 1 : 20 000 000

0   200   400   600   800   1000 km

1 centimetre on the map represents
200 kilometres on the ground

ARCTIC OCEAN

ATLANTIC OCEAN

ICELAND
Reykjavik

NORWAY
SWEDEN
FINLAND
Oslo
Stockholm
Helsinki

RUSSIAN FEDERATION
St. Petersburg
Tallinn
ESTONIA
LATVIA
Riga
Moscow
LITHUANIA
Vilnius
R.F.
Minsk
R. Dvina
BELARUS

UNITED KINGDOM
Edinburgh
Belfast
REPUBLIC OF IRELAND
Dublin
Cardiff
London

DENMARK
Copenhagen
North Sea
Hamburg
Berlin
NETH.
Amsterdam
Rotterdam
Brussels
BEL.
Bonn
LUX.
GERMANY

POLAND
Warsaw
R. Vistula

UKRAINE
Kiev
R. Dnieper

Paris
R. Seine
R. Loire
FRANCE
R. Rhine
Munich
Prague
CZECH REP.
Vienna
SLOVAKIA
Bratislava
Budapest
MOLDOVA
Chisinau

Bay of Biscay
Lyon
Berne
SWITZ.
AUSTRIA
HUNGARY
Ljubljana
SL.
Zagreb
CROATIA
ROMANIA
Bucharest

Oporto
PORTUGAL
ANDORRA
Marseille
R. Rhône
Turin
R. Po
Belgrade
R. Danube
Black Sea

Lisbon
Madrid
SPAIN
Barcelona
Corsica
Rome
ITALY
B.H.
Sarajevo
YUGO-SLAVIA
BULGARIA
Sofia
TURKEY
Istanbul

Valencia
Sardinia
Naples
ALBANIA
Tiranë
Skopje
MAC.

Gibraltar (U.K.)
Palermo
Sicily
GREECE
Athens

Mediterranean Sea
MALTA

AFRICA

ASIA

NORTH
AMERICA

ARCTIC OCEAN

Scale 1 : 20 000 000

| 0 | 200 | 400 | 600 | 800 | 1000 km |

1 centimetre on the map represents
200 kilometres on the ground

Arctic Circle

Key

3000 - 5000 metres
2000 - 3000 metres
1000 - 2000 metres
500 - 1000 metres
200 - 500 metres
0 - 200 metres

Lake

852 ▲ Mountain height
(height in metres)

Snaefell
1833 ▲

ATLANTIC

OCEAN

S c a n d i n a v i a

Gulf of Bothnia

Glittertind
2470 ▲

L. Onega

L. Ladoga

British
Isles

Ben Nevis
1343 ▲

North
Sea

Baltic Sea

R. Volga

R. Dvina

R. Dnieper

R. Don

R. Thames

R. Elbe

English Channel

R. Rhine

R. Vistula

R. Dnieper

R. Seine

R. Loire

R. Danube

Carpathian Mts.

Bay of
Biscay

Mont Blanc
4807 ▲

A L P S

Dolomites

R. Rhône

R. Po

R. Sava

R. Douro

Pyrenées

Adriatic Sea

R. Danube

Black Sea

R. Tagus

Corsica

Vesuvius
1277 ▲

Balearic Is.

Sardinia

A S I A

Sierra Nevada

Mt. Etna
3340 ▲

M e d i t e r r a n e a n   S e a

Sicily

Crete

A F R I C A

35

France is the second largest country in Europe. It has four main rivers, the Seine, Loire, Rhône and Garonne. The highest mountain peaks are in the Alps and the Pyrénées.

France is famous for food and wine. Industries include metals, chemicals, cars and aircraft. Over three quarters of the electricity produced in France comes from nuclear power stations. Modern high speed trains link the main cities.

Grapes ripen in the warm summer weather.

FRANCE

FRANCE

FACT*file*

Population: 57 000 000
Capital: Paris
Language: French
Money: Franc

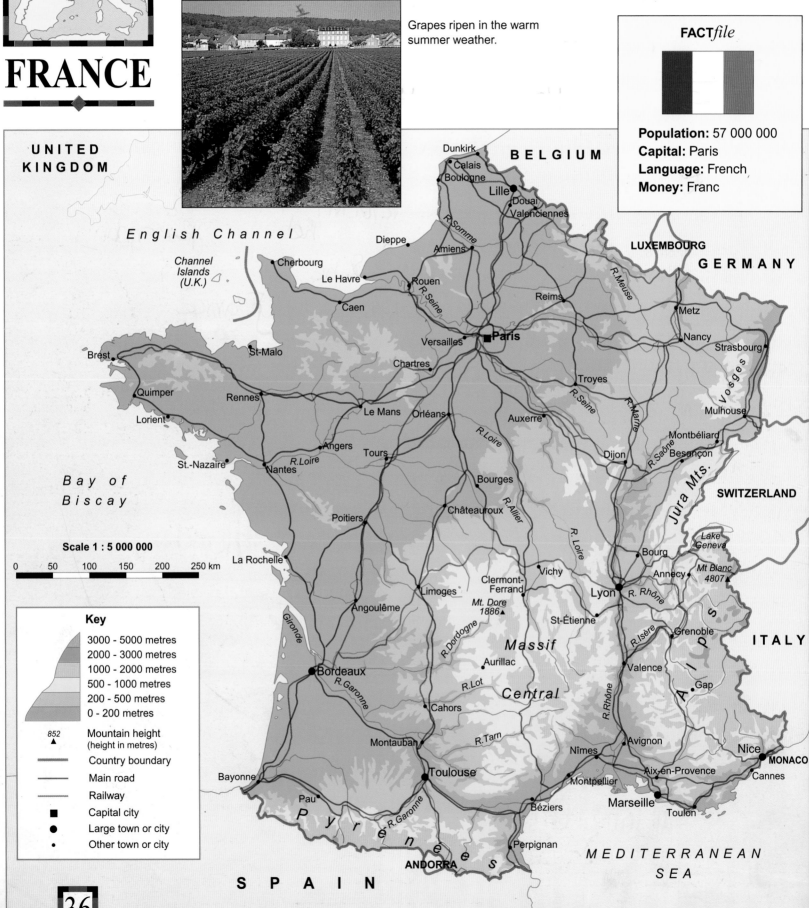

UNITED KINGDOM

BELGIUM

LUXEMBOURG

GERMANY

SWITZERLAND

ITALY

SPAIN

ANDORRA

MONACO

English Channel

Bay of Biscay

MEDITERRANEAN SEA

Channel Islands (U.K.)

Dunkirk
Calais
Boulogne
Lille
Douai
Valenciennes
R.Somme
Dieppe
Amiens
Cherbourg
Le Havre
Rouen
R.Seine
Caen
Reims
R.Meuse
Metz
Nancy
Strasbourg
Paris
Versailles
Chartres
Troyes
R.Seine
R.Marne
Vosges
Mulhouse
Montbéliard
Brest
St-Malo
Auxerre
R.Saône
Besançon
Quimper
Rennes
Le Mans
Orléans
R.Loire
Dijon
Jura Mts.
Lorient
Lake Geneva
Angers
Tours
R.Loire
Bourges
Mt Blanc 4807
St.-Nazaire
Nantes
R.Loire
Bourg
Annecy
Poitiers
Châteauroux
R.Allier
R.Loire
La Rochelle
Clermont-Ferrand
Vichy
Lyon
R.Rhône
Grenoble
Limoges
St-Étienne
Angoulême
Mt. Dore 1886
R.Isère
Valence
Gironde
Massif
Aurillac
R.Dordogne
Gap
Bordeaux
R.Garonne
R.Lot
Central
R.Rhône
Alps
Cahors
Montauban
R.Tarn
Avignon
Nice
Bayonne
Toulouse
Nîmes
Aix-en-Provence
MONACO
Pau
Montpellier
Cannes
R.Garonne
Béziers
Marseille
Toulon
Pyrénées
Perpignan

Scale 1 : 5 000 000

0   50   100   150   200   250 km

Key

- 3000 - 5000 metres
- 2000 - 3000 metres
- 1000 - 2000 metres
- 500 - 1000 metres
- 200 - 500 metres
- 0 - 200 metres

852 ▲ Mountain height (height in metres)

Country boundary

Main road

Railway

■ Capital city

● Large town or city

• Other town or city

Germany has the largest population of any country in Europe. Most Germans live in towns and cities. A lot of people work in banks and offices. Factories make machines, chemicals and cars such as Volkswagen, Mercedes and BMW.

The Rhine, Danube, Elbe and Weser are the main rivers. They flow through the mountains of central and southern Germany. Northern Germany is very flat. The weather in Germany is often similar to the United Kingdom but there is usually more snow in the winter.

GERMANY

FACT*file*

Population: 81 000 000
Capital: Berlin
Language: German
Money: Mark

There are many large forests in southern Germany.

East and West Germany were united when the Berlin Wall was knocked down in 1989.

Scale 1 : 5 000 000

0   50   100   150   200   250 km

DENMARK

Baltic Sea

North Sea

Kiel
Rostock
Lübeck
Cuxhaven
Schwerin
Wilhelmshaven
Bremerhaven
Hamburg
R.Elbe
Oldenburg
Wittenberge
POLAND
Bremen
R.Ems
Hanover
Wolfsburg
Potsdam
Berlin
NETHERLANDS
Osnabrück
Braunschweig
Magdeburg
Münster
Bielefeld
R.Weser
R.Spree
Hamm
Cottbus
R.Rhine
Dortmund
Göttingen
R.Saale
Leipzig
Duisburg
Essen
R.Ruhr
R.Elbe
Mönchen-gladbach
Düsseldorf
Kassel
Dresden
Cologne
Erfurt
Gera
Chemnitz
Aachen
Bonn
Jena
BELGIUM
Zwickau
Koblenz
LUXEMBOURG
Frankfurt
R.Main
CZECH REPUBLIC
R.Mosel
Mainz
Bamberg
Trier
Würzburg
Mannheim
Nürnberg
Bohemian Forest
Saarbrucken
Heidelberg
Rachel 1452
R.Rhine
Regensburg
Karlsruhe
Ingolstadt
Stuttgart
FRANCE
R.Danube
Ulm
Augsburg
Black Forest
Freiburg
Munich
Lake Constance
Zugspitze 2963
LIECHTEN-STEIN
AUSTRIA
SWITZERLAND
ITALY
SLOVENIA

Key

2000 - 3000 metres	Country boundary
1000 - 2000 metres	Main road
500 - 1000 metres	Railway
200 - 500 metres	■ Capital city
0 - 200 metres	● Large town or city
852 ▲ Mountain height (height in metres)	• Other town or city

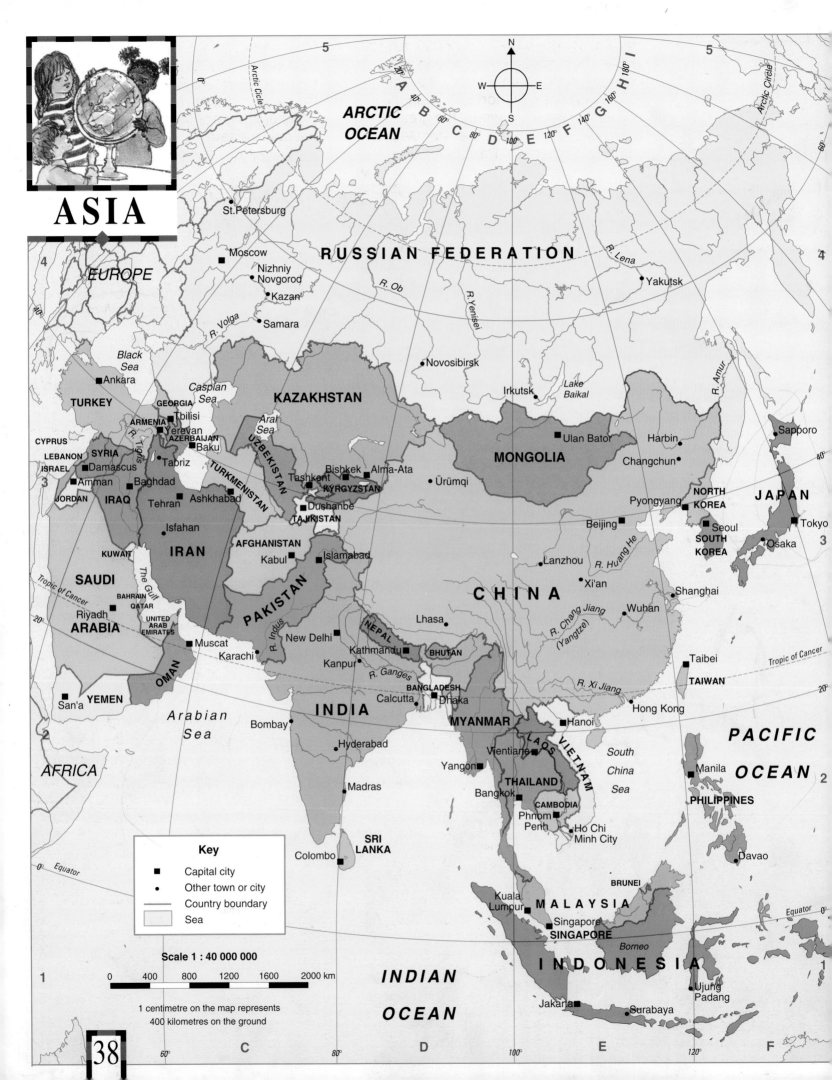

ASIA

ARCTIC OCEAN

N W E S

RUSSIAN FEDERATION

EUROPE

St.Petersburg
Moscow
Nizhniy Novgorod
Kazan
Samara
R. Volga
R. Ob
R. Yenisei
R. Lena
Yakutsk
Novosibirsk
Irkutsk
Lake Baikal
R. Amur

Black Sea
Ankara
TURKEY
GEORGIA
Tbilisi
ARMENIA
Yerevan
AZERBAIJAN
Baku
Caspian Sea
R. Tigris
Tabriz
KAZAKHSTAN
Aral Sea
UZBEKISTAN
Tashkent
Bishkek
Alma-Ata
KYRGYZSTAN
Ürümqi
MONGOLIA
Ulan Bator
Harbin
Changchun
Sapporo

CYPRUS
LEBANON
SYRIA
Damascus
ISRAEL
Amman
Baghdad
JORDAN
IRAQ
Tehran
Isfahan
IRAN
Ashkhabad
TURKMENISTAN
Dushanbe
TAJIKISTAN
AFGHANISTAN
Kabul
Islamabad
Lanzhou
Lhasa
Beijing
Xi'an
NORTH KOREA
Pyongyang
JAPAN
Tokyo
Seoul
SOUTH KOREA
Osaka
CHINA
R. Huang He
Shanghai
Wuhan
R. Chang Jiang (Yangtze)

KUWAIT
SAUDI ARABIA
BAHRAIN
QATAR
Riyadh
UNITED ARAB EMIRATES
The Gulf
PAKISTAN
R. Indus
New Delhi
NEPAL
Kathmandu
BHUTAN
Kanpur
R. Ganges
Muscat
OMAN
Karachi
Taibei
TAIWAN
R. Xi Jiang
Tropic of Cancer
San'a
YEMEN
Arabian Sea
INDIA
Bombay
Hyderabad
BANGLADESH
Calcutta
Dhaka
Hong Kong
MYANMAR
Hanoi
LAOS
VIETNAM
South China Sea
PACIFIC OCEAN

AFRICA
Madras
Yangon
Vientiane
THAILAND
Bangkok
CAMBODIA
Phnom Penh
Ho Chi Minh City
Manila
PHILIPPINES
Davao

SRI LANKA
Colombo

BRUNEI
Kuala Lumpur
MALAYSIA
Singapore
SINGAPORE
Borneo
INDONESIA
Ujung Padang
Jakarta
Surabaya

Equator
INDIAN OCEAN

Key

■ Capital city
• Other town or city
— Country boundary
☐ Sea

Scale 1 : 40 000 000

0 400 800 1200 1600 2000 km

1 centimetre on the map represents
400 kilometres on the ground

Tropic of Cancer
Arctic Circle
Equator

38

India has a population of over 900 million people. The most densely populated areas are along the coast and the plain of the river Ganges. In northern India the land rises upwards towards the great Himalayas. In the west, the Thar Desert forms the border with Pakistan.

Most parts of India are much warmer than the United Kingdom. From June to October the monsoon rains bring water to the parched earth. Rice is the most widespread crop. Coal and iron ore are the main mineral resources.

INDIA

Dams are being built on the river Narmada to provide electricity and water for crops, but the scheme is very expensive and thousands of people will lose their homes in the floods.

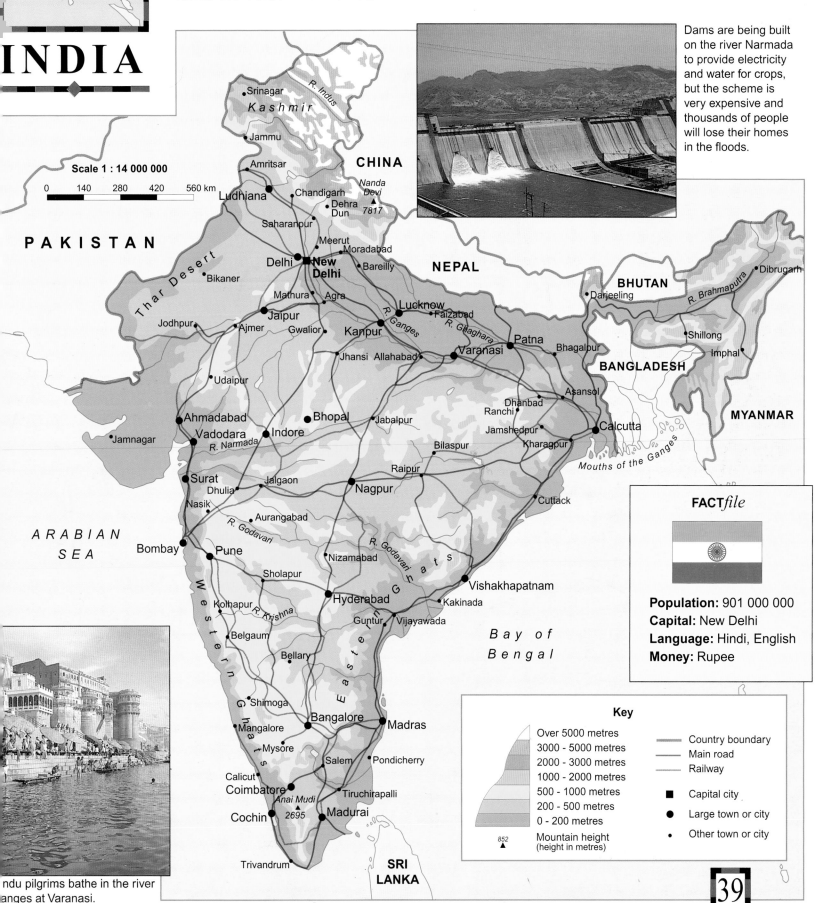

Hindu pilgrims bathe in the river Ganges at Varanasi.

Scale 1 : 14 000 000

0   140   280   420   560 km

PAKISTAN

CHINA

NEPAL

BHUTAN

BANGLADESH

MYANMAR

ARABIAN SEA

Bay of Bengal

SRI LANKA

Kashmir

Thar Desert

Western Ghats

Eastern Ghats

Mouths of the Ganges

R. Indus
R. Ganges
R. Ghaghara
R. Brahmaputra
R. Narmada
R. Godavari
R. Godavari
R. Krishna

Srinagar
Jammu
Amritsar
Ludhiana
Chandigarh
Dehra Dun
Nanda Devi 7817
Saharanpur
Meerut
Moradabad
Delhi
New Delhi
Bareilly
Bikaner
Mathura
Agra
Lucknow
Faizabad
Jaipur
Jodhpur
Ajmer
Gwalior
Kanpur
Jhansi
Allahabad
Varanasi
Patna
Bhagalpur
Darjeeling
Shillong
Imphal
Dibrugarh
Udaipur
Dhanbad
Ranchi
Asansol
Ahmadabad
Bhopal
Jabalpur
Jamshedpur
Calcutta
Vadodara
Indore
Jamnagar
Bilaspur
Kharagpur
Surat
Jalgaon
Raipur
Nagpur
Cuttack
Dhulia
Nasik
Aurangabad
Bombay
Pune
Nizamabad
Sholapur
Kolhapur
Hyderabad
Vishakhapatnam
Belgaum
Guntur
Vijayawada
Kakinada
Bellary
Shimoga
Bangalore
Madras
Mangalore
Mysore
Salem
Pondicherry
Calicut
Coimbatore
Anai Mudi 2695
Tiruchirapalli
Cochin
Madurai
Trivandrum

FACTfile

Population: 901 000 000
Capital: New Delhi
Language: Hindi, English
Money: Rupee

Key

Over 5000 metres
3000 - 5000 metres
2000 - 3000 metres
1000 - 2000 metres
500 - 1000 metres
200 - 500 metres
0 - 200 metres

852 ▲ Mountain height (height in metres)

Country boundary
Main road
Railway

■ Capital city
● Large town or city
• Other town or city

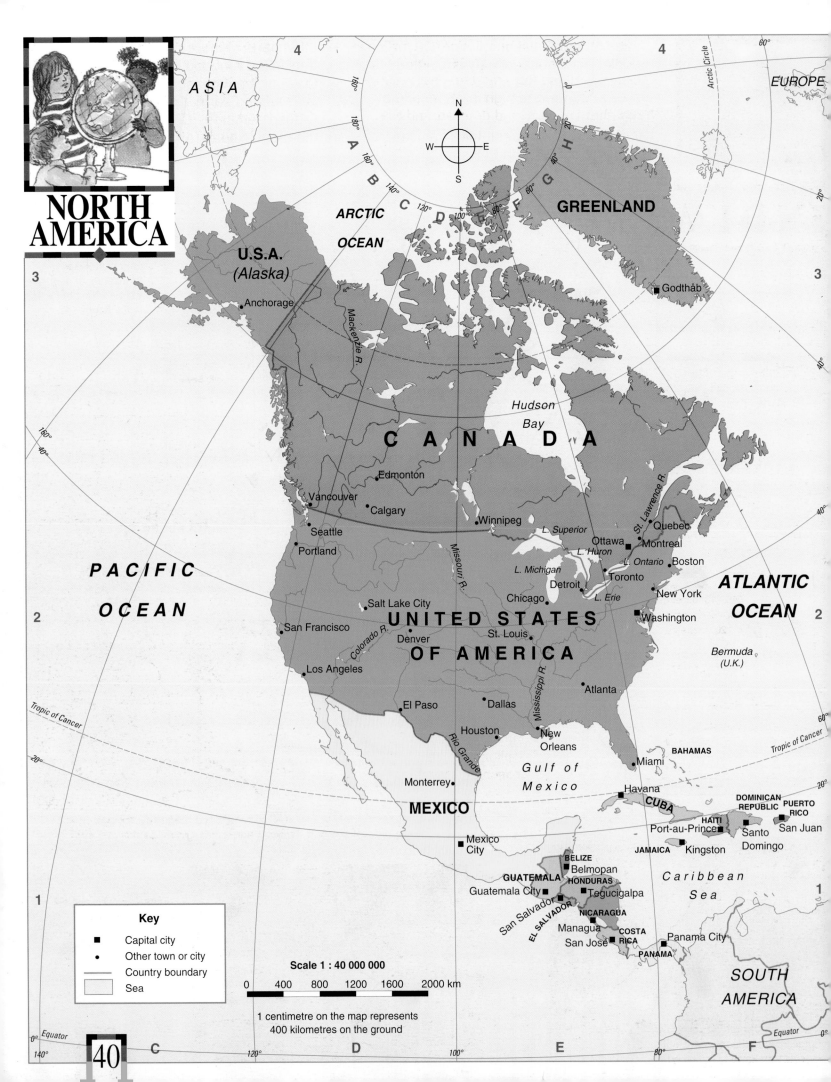

Jamaica is an island in the Caribbean Sea about half the size of Wales. Mountains cross Jamaica from east to west reaching over 2000 metres high in places. The weather is hotter and drier around the coast than in the mountains.

Tourists come to Jamaica to visit the beaches and enjoy the sunshine. Coffee, sugar and fruits are grown for sale to other countries. South of Ocho Rios there are large mines producing bauxite. Aluminium is made from this mineral.

JAMAICA

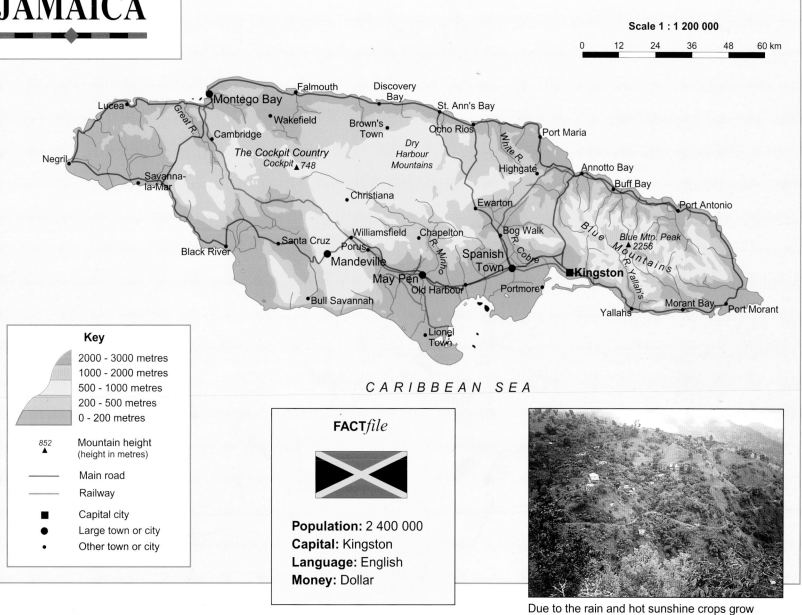

Scale 1 : 1 200 000

0   12   24   36   48   60 km

Lucea • Montego Bay • Falmouth • Discovery Bay • St. Ann's Bay • Port Maria
Great R.
Negril • Wakefield • Brown's Town • Ocho Rios
Cambridge
The Cockpit Country
Cockpit ▲748
Dry Harbour Mountains
Highgate
Annotto Bay
Buff Bay
Savanna-la-Mar
Christiana
Port Antonio
Black River • Santa Cruz • Williamsfield • Chapelton • Bog Walk
Porus • Mandeville • R. Minho • Spanish Town • R. Cobre • Kingston
Blue Mtn. Peak ▲2256
Blue Mountains
Ewarton
May Pen • Old Harbour • Portmore
Bull Savannah
Lionel Town
Yallahs • Morant Bay • Port Morant

CARIBBEAN SEA

Key

	2000 - 3000 metres
	1000 - 2000 metres
	500 - 1000 metres
	200 - 500 metres
	0 - 200 metres

852 ▲   Mountain height (height in metres)

——————   Main road

——————   Railway

■   Capital city

●   Large town or city

•   Other town or city

FACTfile

Population: 2 400 000
Capital: Kingston
Language: English
Money: Dollar

Due to the rain and hot sunshine crops grow quickly, and dense, green vegetation covers the hillsides.

Large cruise ships visit Jamaica with tourists from around the world.

In 1988 Hurricane Gilbert brought widespread destruction to Jamaica. At Kingston International Airport aircraft were blown over and destroyed.

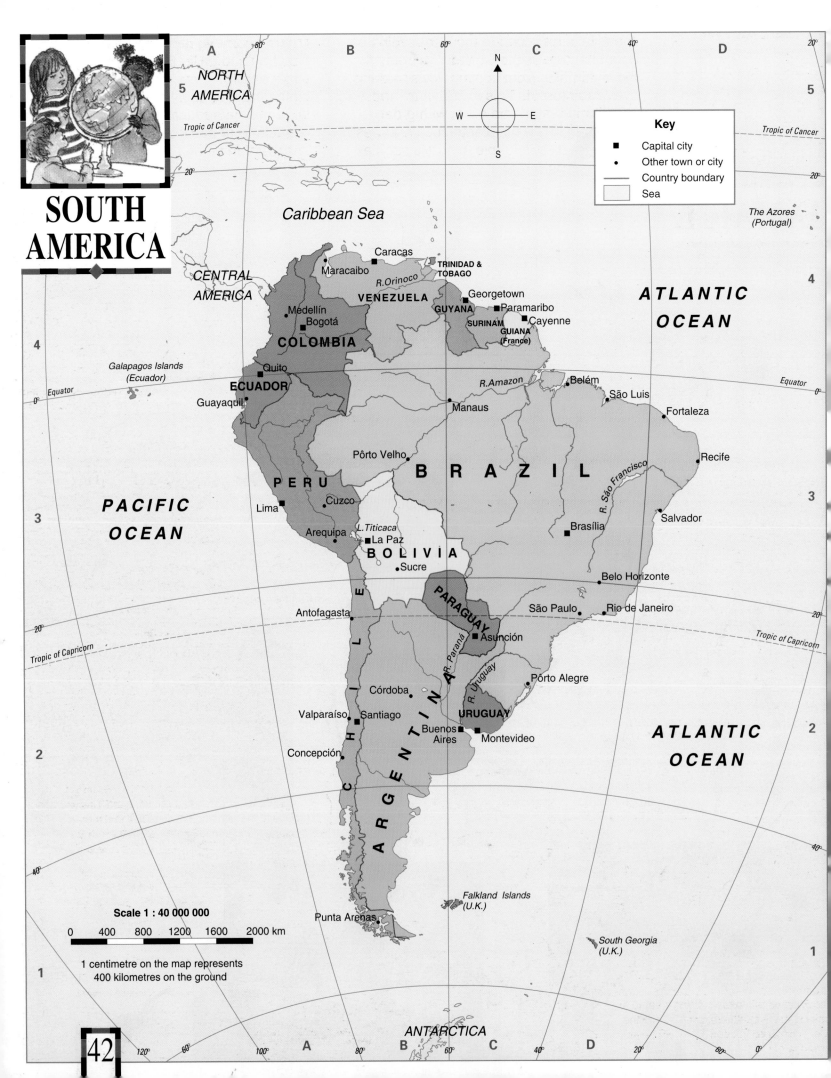

SOUTH AMERICA

NORTH AMERICA

Tropic of Cancer

CENTRAL AMERICA

Caribbean Sea

Galapagos Islands (Ecuador)

Equator

PACIFIC OCEAN

Tropic of Capricorn

ATLANTIC OCEAN

The Azores (Portugal)

ATLANTIC OCEAN

ANTARCTICA

Key
- ■ Capital city
- • Other town or city
- — Country boundary
- ▭ Sea

Caracas
Maracaibo
R.Orinoco
VENEZUELA
Georgetown
GUYANA
Paramaribo
SURINAM
Cayenne
GUIANA (France)
TRINIDAD & TOBAGO
Medellín
Bogotá
COLOMBIA
Quito
ECUADOR
Guayaquil
R.Amazon
Belém
São Luis
Fortaleza
Manaus

P E R U
Cuzco
Lima
Arequipa
L.Titicaca
La Paz
B O L I V I A
Sucre

Pôrto Velho

B R A Z I L
R.São Francisco
Recife
Salvador
Brasília
Belo Horizonte

Antofagasta
PARAGUAY
Asunción
R.Paraná
São Paulo
Rio de Janeiro

Córdoba
Valparaíso
Santiago
Concepción

C H I L E
A R G E N T I N A
R.Uruguay
URUGUAY
Pôrto Alegre
Buenos Aires
Montevideo

Punta Arenas

Falkland Islands (U.K.)

South Georgia (U.K.)

Scale 1 : 40 000 000

0   400   800   1200   1600   2000 km

1 centimetre on the map represents
400 kilometres on the ground

BRAZIL

Brazil is a vast country more than thirty times the size of the United Kingdom. In the north, the river Amazon flows through dense rainforest. This is one of the most important habitats on earth with great numbers of different plants and creatures. There are also valuable minerals such as gold and iron ore.

Most people live near the Atlantic coast. São Paulo and Rio de Janeiro are the largest cities. Cars, aircraft, shoes and clothes are made in the factories. Crops grown for sale to other countries include coffee, sugar and maize. Cattle raising is important in many places.

FACT*file*

Population: 151 000 000
Capital: Brasília
Language: Portuguese
Money: Cruzeiro

São Paulo is one of the largest cities in the world with a population of more than 15 million people.

The Amazon rainforest is being cleared to make space for cattle ranches. Once the trees have been cut down they will never grow again.

Key

2000 - 3000 metres
1000 - 2000 metres
500 - 1000 metres
200 - 500 metres
0 - 200 metres

852 ▲ Mountain height (height in metres)

Country boundary

Main road

Railway

■ Capital city

● Large town or city

• Other town or city

Scale 1 : 25 000 000

0   250   500   750   1000   1250 km

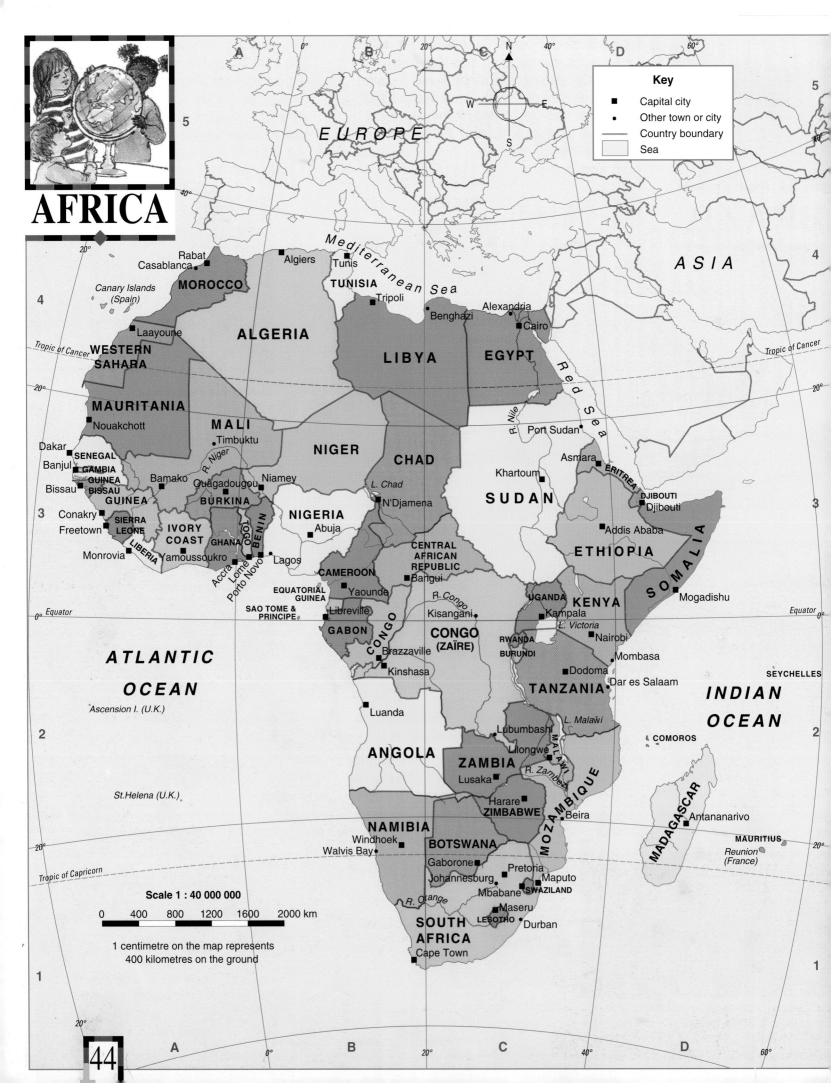

AFRICA

Key
- ■ Capital city
- • Other town or city
- — Country boundary
- □ Sea

EUROPE

ASIA

Mediterranean Sea

Rabat • Casablanca
Algiers
Tunis
TUNISIA
Tripoli
Benghazi
Alexandria
Cairo

MOROCCO

Canary Islands (Spain)

Laayoune

WESTERN SAHARA

ALGERIA

LIBYA

EGYPT

Red Sea

Tropic of Cancer

MAURITANIA

Nouakchott

MALI

• Timbuktu

NIGER

CHAD

R. Nile
Port Sudan

Asmara
ERITREA

Dakar
SENEGAL
Banjul **GAMBIA**
Bissau **GUINEA BISSAU**
GUINEA

Bamako
Ouagadougou
Niamey
BURKINA

L. Chad
N'Djamena

Khartoum

SUDAN

DJIBOUTI
Djibouti

Addis Ababa

Conakry
Freetown **SIERRA LEONE**
IVORY COAST
GHANA
Yamoussoukro
Accra
Lome
Porto Novo
TOGO
BENIN

NIGERIA
Abuja •
Lagos

CENTRAL AFRICAN REPUBLIC
Bangui •

ETHIOPIA

SOMALIA

Mogadishu

Monrovia
LIBERIA

CAMEROON
Yaounde ■

EQUATORIAL GUINEA

SAO TOME & PRINCIPE

Libreville ■

R. Congo
Kisangani •

UGANDA
Kampala ■
KENYA

L. Victoria
Nairobi •

Mombasa •

Equator

GABON

CONGO

CONGO (ZAÏRE)

Brazzaville ■
Kinshasa ■

RWANDA
BURUNDI

Dodoma ■
Dar es Salaam

SEYCHELLES

ATLANTIC OCEAN

Ascension I. (U.K.)

Luanda ■

INDIAN OCEAN

TANZANIA

Lubumbashi •
L. Malaŵi

COMOROS

St. Helena (U.K.)

ANGOLA

Lilongwe ■
MALAWI

ZAMBIA
Lusaka ■

R. Zambezi

MOZAMBIQUE

Harare ■
ZIMBABWE
Beira •

MADAGASCAR

Antananarivo •

MAURITIUS

NAMIBIA

Windhoek ■
Walvis Bay •

BOTSWANA

Reunion (France)

Tropic of Capricorn

Scale 1 : 40 000 000

0 400 800 1200 1600 2000 km

1 centimetre on the map represents
400 kilometres on the ground

Gaborone ■
Johannesburg •
Mbabane ■
Maseru ■
LESOTHO

Pretoria ■
Maputo ■
SWAZILAND

Durban •

R. Orange

SOUTH AFRICA
Cape Town ■

KENYA

Kenya is about twice the size of the United Kingdom and lies across the equator. Mount Kenya is the highest peak. There are deserts in the north, savanna grasslands in the south and white sandy beaches along the coast.

Maize is the main food crop for local people. Tea, coffee, sugar and pineapples are sold to other countries. Thousands of tourists travel to Kenya to see the lions, rhinos, elephants and other animals in the game parks.

FACTfile

Population: 28 000 000
Capital: Nairobi
Language: Swahili, English
Money: Shilling

Game parks help to conserve rare animals such as the black rhino, but local people have been driven out of the reserves.

Mount Kenya is an extinct volcano rising to a height of 5199 metres.

Scale 1 : 6 000 000

0   60   120   180   240   300 km

Key

Over 5000 metres
3000 - 5000 metres
2000 - 3000 metres
1000 - 2000 metres
500 - 1000 metres
200 - 500 metres
0 - 200 metres

852 ▲ Mountain height (height in metres)

‒‒‒ Seasonal river

Country boundary
Main road
Railway

■ Capital city
● Large town or city
• Other town or city

SUDAN

ETHIOPIA

UGANDA

SOMALIA

TANZANIA

INDIAN OCEAN

Lake Turkana

Rift Valley

R. Turkwel

R. Kerio

Lodwar

Marsabit

Wajir

R. Laga Bor

R. Lagh Bogal

▲ Mt Elgon 4321

Kitale

Eldoret

Busia

Butere

Kakamega

Kisumu

Solai

R. Ewaso Ngiro

Isiolo

Meru

R. Tana

Nyahururu

Nanyuki

▲ Mt Kenya 5199

Nakuru

Aberdare Range

Kericho

Kisii

Mau Hills

Nyeri

Embu

Garissa

Lake Victoria

Thika

Kangondi

Nairobi

Machakos

R. Thua

Galole

R. Tana

Magadi

R. Sabaki

Voi

Malindi

Mombasa

OCEANIA

N
W   E
S

Tropic of Cancer

20°

120°

OCEANIA

Oceania is a group of islands scattered across the south Pacific Ocean. Many of these attractive islands have become known to Europeans only in the last few hundred years.

The largest island, Australia, is one of the world's largest countries but has only about 17 million people. The largest towns and cities are along the coast. Most of the country is made up of desert and scrubland. There are many sheep and cattle farms which cover vast areas of land.

P A C I F I C

O C E A N

A S I A

KIRIBATI

Equator

Madang

PAPUA NEW GUINEA

SOLOMON ISLANDS

Port Moresby

Honiara

T i m o r   S e a

Darwin

C o r a l

VANUATU

FIJI

Cooktown

S e a

Vila

Suva

Townsville

New Caledonia (France)

Nouméa

20°

Tropic of Capricorn

Alice Springs

Rockhampton

Tropic of Capricorn

A U S T R A L I A

Brisbane

Kalgoorlie

L. Eyre

R. Darling

Perth

Newcastle
Sydney

Adelaide

R. Murray

Canberra

Auckland

Melbourne

T a s m a n

NEW ZEALAND

S e a

Wellington

Key

■   Capital city

●   Other town or city

Christchurch

Hobart

──   Country boundary

     Sea

Dunedin

Scale 1 : 35 000 000

0   350   700   1050   1400   1750 km

1 centimetre on the map represents
350 kilometres on the ground

ANTARCTICA

Antarctica circles the South Pole, and is the coldest and windiest place on earth.

Scientists go to this continent to study the rocks, weather and wildlife.

0°

Antarctic Circle

Southern Ocean

Atlantic Ocean

Weddel Sea

Ronne Ice Shelf

Bellinghausen Sea

90°W

Vinson Massif

SOUTH POLE

Mt. Menzies

90°E

Vostok

Mt. Kirkpatrick

Amundsen Sea

Ross Ice Shelf

Mt. Erebus

Pacific Ocean

180°

Scale 1 : 40 000 000

Key

Ice shelf	
Mountains	
Highest peaks	
Scientific base	

Beneath the ice there are rich supplies of coal, oil and metal ore. Some countries have tried to claim these for themselves.

Around the coast there are large numbers of seals, penguins and fish which can survive the harsh conditions.

Cross-section through Antarctica

Antarctica is covered by a vast sheet of ice. At the edges, great ice-bergs as tall as sky-scrapers break off and float out to sea.

Western Ice Sheet

sea level

Eastern Ice Sheet

pack ice and icebergs

Underlying rocks

Location of cross-section

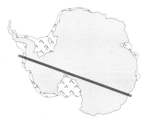

47

INDEX

An atlas index is a list of map names.

Most of the names shown in the atlas are listed in the index. There are separate files for a) countries, b) rivers, c) seas and lakes, d) towns and cities and e) mountains and deserts. Each file is arranged in alphabetical order.

To find a place or a landscape feature in the atlas, first look for its name in the correct index file. You will then discover the page you need. You will also find the grid code or reference.

Using the grid code.

The grid code consists of a letter and a number. The letter tells you which column to look at and the number tells you the row. Look in the square where they cross for the place or feature you want to find. For example :

Cape Town 44 B1

How to find Cape Town using the atlas index.

1. Look up the entry in the towns and cities file.

    Cape Town 44 B1
    ↑   ↑   ↑
    name   page grid code

2. Turn to the correct page.

3. Find the grid square.

How to find Cape Town using the atlas index.

COUNTRIES

Afghanistan 38 C3
Albania 34 C2
Algeria 44 A4
Angola 44 B2
Argentina 42 B1
Armenia 38 B4
Australia 46 B2
Austria 34 C2
Azerbaijan 38 B4

Bangladesh 38 D3
Belarus 34 D2
Belgium 34 C2
Belize 40 E1
Benin 44 B3
Bolivia 42 B3
Bosnia-Herzegovina 34 C2
Botswana 44 C1
Brazil 42 B3
Bulgaria 34 D2
Burkina 44 A3
Burundi 44 C2

Cambodia 38 E2
Cameroon 44 B3
Canada 40 D3
Central African Republic 44 B3
Chad 44 B3
Chile 42 B2
China 38 D3
Colombia 42 B4
Congo 44 B2
Congo (Zaïre) 44 C2
Costa Rica 40 E1

Croatia 34 C2
Cuba 40 F2
Cyprus 38 A3
Czech Republic 34 C2

Denmark 34 C2
Djibouti 44 D3
Dominican Republic 40 F1

Ecuador 42 B3
Egypt 44 C4
El Salvador 40 E1
Equatorial Guinea 44 B3
Eritrea 44 D3
Estonia 34 D2
Ethiopia 44 C3

Finland 34 D3
France 34 C2

Gabon 44 B2
Gambia 44 A3
Georgia 38 B4
Germany 34 C2
Ghana 44 A3
Greece 34 D1
Greenland 40 G4
Guatemala 40 E1
Guiana 42 C4
Guinea 44 A3
Guinea Bissau 44 A3
Guyana 42 C4

Honduras 40 E1
Hungary 34 C2

Iceland 34 B3
India 38 C3

Indonesia 38 E1
Iran 38 B3
Iraq 38 B3
Ireland 34 B2
Israel 38 A3
Italy 34 C2
Ivory Coast 44 A3

Jamaica 40 F1
Japan 38 F3
Jordan 38 A3

Kazakhstan 38 C4
Kenya 44 C3
Kuwait 38 B3
Kyrgyzstan 38 C4

Laos 38 E2
Latvia 34 D2
Lebanon 38 A3
Lesotho 44 C1
Liberia 44 A3
Libya 44 B4
Lithuania 34 D2
Luxembourg 34 C2

Macedonia 34 D2
Madagascar 44 D1
Malawi 44 C2
Malaysia 38 E2
Mali 44 A3
Mauritania 44 A3
Mexico 40 D2
Moldova 34 D2
Mongolia 38 D4
Morocco 44 A4
Mozambique 44 C1
Myanmar 38 D3

Namibia 44 B1
Nepal 38 D3
Netherlands 34 C2
New Zealand 46 D2
Nicaragua 40 E1
Niger 44 B3
Nigeria 44 B3
North Korea 38 F4
Norway 34 C3

Oman 38 B2

Pakistan 38 C3
Panama 40 E1
Papua New Guinea 46 C3
Paraguay 42 B2
Peru 42 B3
Philippines 38 F2
Poland 34 C2
Portugal 34 B1

Romania 34 D2
Russian Federation 38 B5
Rwanda 44 C2

Sao Tomé and Principe 44 B3
Saudi Arabia 38 B3
Senegal 44 A3
Sierra Leone 44 A3
Singapore 38 E2
Slovakia 34 C2
Slovenia 34 C2
Somalia 44 D3
South Africa 44 C1
South Korea 38 F3
Spain 34 B1
Sri Lanka 38 D2

Sudan 44 C3
Surinam 42 C4
Swaziland 44 C1
Sweden 34 C3
Switzerland 34 C2
Syria 38 A3

Taiwan 38 F3
Tajikistan 38 C3
Tanzania 44 C2
Thailand 38 E2
Togo 44 B3
Tunisia 44 B4
Turkey 38 A3
Turkmenistan 38 B3

Uganda 44 C3
Ukraine 34 D2
United Arab Emirates 38 B3
United Kingdom 34 B2
United States of America 40 D3
Uruguay 42 C2
Uzbekistan 38 B4

Vanuatu 46 D3
Venezuela 42 B4
Vietnam 38 E2

Western Sahara 44 A4

Yemen 38 B2
Yugoslavia 34 D2

Zambia 44 C2
Zimbabwe 44 C2

MOUNTAINS AND DESERTS

Aconcagua 4 D2
Alps 35 C2
Andes 4 D3
Appalachian Mountains 4 D5
Atlas Mountains 4 F5
Carpathian Mountains 35 D2
Ethiopian Highlands 5 H4

Gobi Desert 5 J5
Himalayas 5 I5
Kilimanjaro 5 H3
Kunlun Shan 5 I5
Mont Blanc 35 C2
Mount Everest 5 I4
Mount McKinley 4 B6
Puntjak Jaya 5 K3
Pyrénées 35 D2
Rocky Mountains 4 C5
Sahara Desert 4 F4
Ural Mountains 5 H6

SEAS AND LAKES

Adriatic Sea 35 C2
Arabian Sea 38 C2
Aral Sea 38 B4
Arctic Ocean 5 J6
Atlantic Ocean 4 E4
Baltic Sea 35 C2
Bay of Biscay 35 B2
Bering Sea 5 L5
Black Sea 35 D2
Caribbean Sea 40 F1
Caspian Sea 38 B4
Coral Sea 46 C3

East China Sea 5 K4
Great Lakes 4 D5
Gulf of Bothnia 35 C3
Gulf of Mexico 40 E2
Hudson Bay 40 E4
Indian Ocean 5 I3
Lake Baikal 38 E4
Lake Chad 44 B3
Lake Erie 40 E3
Lake Eyre 46 B2
Lake Huron 40 E3
Lake Ladoga 35 D3
Lake Malawi 44 C2
Lake Michigan 40 E3
Lake Onega 35 D3

Lake Ontario 40 F3
Lake Superior 40 E3
Lake Tanganyika 5 G3
Lake Titicaca 42 B3
Lake Victoria 44 C2
Mediterranean Sea 35 C1
North Sea 35 C2
Pacific Ocean 4 C4
Red Sea 44 C4
South China Sea 5 J4
Southern Ocean 5 I2
Tasman Sea 46 C2
Timor Sea 46 A3